Gibson Girls *and* Suffragists

PERCEPTIONS OF WOMEN FROM 1900 TO 1918

Catherine Gourley

Twenty-First Century Books • Minneapolis

For Mom. You would have liked this one.

Twenty-First Century Books
A division of Lerner Publishing Group, Inc.
241 First Avenue North
Minneapolis, MN 55401 U.S.A.

Website address: www.lernerbooks.com

Library of Congress Cataloging-in-Publication Data

Gourley, Catherine, 1950–
    Gibson girls and suffragists perceptions of women from 1900 to 1918 / by Catherine Gourley.
       p.   cm. — (Images and issues of women in the Twentieth Century)
    Includes bibliographical references and index.
    ISBN 978–0–8225–7150–6 (lib. bdg. : alk. paper)
    1. Women—United States—History—20th century. 2. Women—United States—Social conditions—20th century.
  3. Women—United States—Social life and customs—20th century. I. Title.
    HQ1419.G68 2008
    305.40973'09041—dc22   2007001689

Manufactured in the United States of America
1 2 3 4 5 6 – JR – 13 12 11 10 09 08

Contents

At the turn of the nineteenth century,
women were second-class citizens—and
there was not much they could do about it
since they did not have the right to vote.

AUTHOR'S NOTE

Why do they look angry? I wondered. The few photographs (for there weren't many) of the nineteenth- and early twentieth-century women suffragists I saw while in high school and college showed sour-faced, elderly women scowling into the camera. Through my young-adult eyes, these advocates of women's right to vote weren't fashionable or feminine. And they didn't seem happy.

In the 1960s, when I was in high school, schools didn't teach women's history. History was history, and at the time, I didn't notice that most of the interesting stories were about men. Those few historical photographs of women led me to believe that suffragists were unusual. I thought of them as a stereotype: a small group of bossy and belligerent women. I understood and appreciated that they had succeeded in getting women the right to vote. Without them, I would not have been able to vote in my first presidential election, in 1972. I just didn't want to look like them.

In the 1970s, another wave of feminism spread across the

A 1912 Harry Grant Dart cartoon is an example of the way the media treated the suffragist movement in the early twentieth century. The words poke fun at the suffragists' activities. But the indirect message is that they are a very unappealing group of women.

United States. I rode that wave. Many colleges began to offer courses on women's history. While I had already graduated and was teaching high school, I suddenly realized there was much about women's history that I had never known. I began to look beyond the historical images not just to question what the suffragists had accomplished but also to wonder why a woman became a suffragist and how. I discovered that women of all sizes, shapes, and ages had participated in the suffrage movement, some even as forceful protesters against women getting the vote! I discovered too that I rather liked these feisty women. Even if I didn't want to look like the media image of them, I wanted to be like them.

In researching this book, the first in a series on women's images and issues, I traveled back in time and studied images of other women and not just the suffragists. I found those images in photographs and magazine illustrations, on the covers of parlor sheet music, and in the headlines of newspaper articles. Specifically, I hunted for answers to two questions: How did the popular media of the past portray women? Were those images of women accurate or misleading?

Throughout the twentieth century, media images—whether fact or fiction, stereotypical or sensationalized—influenced women's perception of themselves. But the influence was not always blind acceptance. Many women rebelled against the images society painted for them. Their rebellion not only made headlines but also opened doors for other women to express their own individuality. As you read, you too will travel back in time. I hope you'll return to the present with greater understanding of how popular culture may have influenced your mother, your grandmother, and perhaps even your great-grandmother. More important, I hope you'll see yourself reflected within these pages and understand that you—not society—hold the paintbrush that creates the person you become.

—*Catherine Gourley*

LONDON & NORTH WESTERN RAILWAY

Connecting Trains from all Stations to Liverpool and Glasgow for Steamers to United States and Canada en route to CHICAGO.

WORLD'S COLUMBIAN EXPOSITION

THE MACHINERY HALL—COLUMBIAN EXPOSITION
CHICAGO

CHICAGO, 1893

Even more important than the discovery of Columbus is the fact the General (U.S.) Government has just discovered women.

—Bertha Potter Palmer, Board of Lady Managers of the World's Columbian Exposition, October 1892

a century doesn't end in a second,

like a door slamming. Rather, a century turns. It changes a little bit at a time, like wind wafting through an open window. Change lifts the curtains and stirs about the house, hinting at what may come.

The first gust of wind that suggested the turning of the nineteenth century came on May 1, 1893, in Chicago, Illinois. This was the opening day of the spectacular World's Columbian Exposition, also called the Chicago World's Fair. The fair marked the four-hundred-year anniversary of Christopher Columbus's discovery of America in 1492.

World's fairs were popular entertainment in the latter half of the nineteenth century. But the Columbian Exposition was by far the largest. On display throughout the more than 200 acres (81 hectares) of fairgrounds were wonders from all over the world. Fairgoers could stroll down "Cairo Street" and imagine they were in Egypt rather than in the Midwest. They could visit an Eskimo (Inuit) village or a Turkish mosque, an Islamic house of worship. They could admire the work of Japanese umbrella makers or gaze in wonder at a 1,500-pound (680-kilogram) chocolate

The 1893 World's Columbian Exposition grounds (above) were truly magnificent. Artists and architects followed guidelines: all buildings were to be in the classical Greek style, the height of the buildings was not to exceed 60 feet (18 meters), and all buildings were to be painted white. Facing page: A British railway poster touts the World's Fair, 1893.

replica of a famous Greek statue, the Venus de Milo. They might squeal in delight at the snake charmer or blush during the belly dancer's hootchy-kootchy performance (as the press called it).

The fair also showcased the United States' growth throughout the nineteenth century into an industrial nation and world leader. Fairgoers saw the first-ever moving pictures, displayed on a machine called the Kinetoscope invented by Thomas Edison. Some mechanical innovations were large and awe inspiring, such as the first-ever Ferris wheel. The wheel was 250 feet (76 m) high. Each car could hold as many as sixty people. More than two thousand people could ride the wheel at one time! Other mechanical devices on display—the zipper, for example—were small but no less impressive. The fair introduced the world to new kinds of food as well: Cream of Wheat cereal, Aunt Jemima Pancake Mix, a caramel-coated popcorn candy called Cracker Jack, the hamburger, and carbonated soda. Fairgoers could ride on a moving sidewalk or be propelled along newly built canals in an Italian boat called a gondola.

All these wonders—the giant Ferris wheel, the hamburger, and the blazing electric lights—signaled change. So, too, did the Woman's Building.

Never before had a world's fair exhibited women's achievements

Fifty cents would get you two revolutions on the newly invented Ferris wheel. Not recommended for those afraid of crowded spaces or heights, the wheel rolled upward to a height of 250 feet (76 m). Thirty-six wooden cars held sixty people each.

in a building solely their own. When the U.S. Congress had approved the construction of the World's Columbian Exposition, it also created the Board of Lady Managers. With this act of Congress, for the first time, an organization of women had the responsibilities and legal right to conduct business on behalf of the U.S. government. The Board of Lady Managers elected Bertha Potter Palmer as its president. She emphasized the significance of the board when she said, "Even more important than the discovery of Columbus is the fact the General Government has just discovered women."

To understand the significance of this act of Congress, one must first understand what nineteenth-century U.S. society believed about women. Women of that era did not have the right to vote in public elections. Once a woman married, she usually gave up her last name (which was, of course, her father's) and took her husband's surname. The media referred to women not by their names (Bertha Palmer or even Mrs. Bertha Palmer, for example), but by their husband's names (Mrs. Potter Palmer—Potter was her husband's first name). Many men and some women too believed the female was the "weaker sex," not only physically but also emotionally and intellectually. Men were logical. Women were not. A woman's strength was her moral character.

The phrase "true womanhood" appeared often in magazines and advice books of the nineteenth century. A true woman possessed four virtues. She was pious, or religious. She was pure, or chaste in thoughts and in behavior. She was submissive and dependent upon her father or her husband for financial security and protection. Finally, she was domestic. Her place was in the home and

Bertha Honoré Potter Palmer was not only the queen of Chicago society but also very charitable. Her husband, Potter, was twenty-three years older than she. He died in 1902, leaving her his entire estate. His lawyer did not approve and asked, "What if she married again?" Potter Palmer replied, "If she does, he'll need the money."

The Woman's Building of the Columbian Exposition was impressive at 76,000 square feet (7,060 sq. m). Designed in the Italian Renaissance–style at a cost of $140,000, it served as the headquarters for the Board of Lady Managers. The board oversaw the exhibition of women's work throughout the exposition.

not in public business, industry, or politics. The concept of true womanhood placed wife and mother on a pedestal and frowned upon those outrageous females who insisted on stepping down to study or work outside the home. This image of women was idealized, however, since many women held paying jobs out of necessity. To put food on the table or pay the rent, women worked in factories and mills, and as laundresses and maids. Increasingly at the turn of century, they worked in department stores and offices as sales clerks and secretaries.

The Woman's Building of the World's Columbian Exposition in 1893, however, challenged the way the world viewed

women and the way women viewed themselves. The architect of the Woman's Building was twenty-one-year-old Sophia G. Hayden. Hayden's youth was not as startling as was her occupation. During the nineteenth century, in general, most people frowned upon women who studied to become a physician, an engineer, or an architect. There were only a few female architects in the country at the time, and Sophia G. Hayden was one of them.

Above the second story of the Woman's Building were caryatids, or columns in the shape of female figures. The caryatids wore flowing robes like those of the women of ancient Greece. Enid Yandell of Louisville,

Kentucky, sculpted the caryatids. She, too, was quite young—twenty-two. In fact, women designed almost everything about the Woman's Building—the interior decorations, the paintings and tapestries, the carved wooden doors, and the statues beneath the arches. The displays in the parlors and galleries included laces, embroideries, fans, and jewelry that were also the work of women. The library held volumes of books written by women. A modern kitchen and hospital showcased women's domestic and medical abilities.

On May 1, 1893, at two o'clock, the doors to the Woman's Building opened for the first time. Within minutes, every chair was taken by women laced up in corsets (a stiff undergarment) and wearing stiff, high-collared dresses. And still the people entered—their skirts sweeping the marble floor. They wore gloves and elaborate

Within minutes, every chair was taken by women laced up in corsets and wearing stiff, high-collared dresses.

hats with feathers and ribbons. They carried daintily embroidered lace handkerchiefs. The guests stood under the grand arches and in the passageways until even these open spaces were crowded to capacity.

Seated on a temporary stage were prominent women from countries all around the world, including a baroness from Sweden and a princess from Russia. They had come for the opening-day ceremonies. Present, too, in the galleries and parlors were images of noteworthy women from history and from fiction. Portraits of the ancient Greek mathematician Hypatia and the ancient Greek poet Sappho hung on the walls. Sculptures of Psyche, a heroine from Greek mythology, and Maud Muller, a character from a poem by John Greenleaf Whittier, gazed with marble eyes over the gathering.

When it was announced that Mrs. Bertha Potter Palmer was about to speak, a burst of cheers and applause greeted her. Women waved their white handkerchiefs in the air. "Members of the Board of Lady Managers, Ladies and Gentlemen," Palmer began, "The moment of fruition has arrived. The gates of the Columbian Exposition are open." The cheers, the applause, and the flutter of handkerchiefs began again.

"There are those who hold the opinion that woman should be tenderly guarded and cherished within the sacred precincts of the home," she said, her diamonds gleaming in the sunlight. We had been told, she continued, that a woman was "too delicate and nervous to endure the . . . mental strain of the schoolroom. Her brain, being female, wasn't logical and so could not solve mathematical or scientific problems. Who had told women these things? Physicians and scientists and teachers," said Palmer. Why, even parents had told their daughters that "there was nothing that a man so abominated as a learned woman."

"What is to be done with this strong, self-poised creature of glowing imagination and high ideals, who evidently intends as a natural and inherent right to pursue her self-development in her chosen line of work?"

—Bertha Potter Palmer, May 1, 1893

Palmer asked, "What is to be done with this strong, self-poised creature of glowing imagination and high ideals, who evidently intends as a natural and inherent right to pursue her self-development in her chosen line of work? Is the world ready . . . to open all doors before her?" Yes! the sea of fluttering handkerchiefs answered.

"Would you have woman step down from her pedestal in order to enter practical life?" Palmer asked. "Yes! A thousand times yes." Still again, the applause and cheers of the women—and some men too—interrupted her speech. "I am not a believer in the pedestal theory," she laughed. She hoped that the World's Fair and the Woman's Building would clear away misconceptions about women. Women were intelligent. Women were creative. In time, they would break the barriers society had placed around them.

The century was turning, and the United States was changing. American women were changing too. But change doesn't happen all at once. Not everyone in society agreed with Palmer that women should step down from their pedestal. Nor did they agree with Susan B. Anthony or Elizabeth Cady Stanton, who had predicted that women in the coming century would at last win the right to vote. Many in society feared a future where a woman might have rights equal to those of a man. Surely the family would suffer without a woman at home to care for her husband and children, they thought. Business and government, too, could not succeed if a woman—so emotional rather than logical—took charge. These were real fears expressed by both men and women in U.S. society at the turn of the century.

A 1915 cartoon suggests that the only way women could be persuaded to vote is if the ballot box were brought directly to them. Insulting images such as these brought more women to the suffragist movement rather than turning them against it.

Gibson Girls and Suffragists explores the images and issues that commented on and influenced women's lives at the turn of the nineteenth century. It is the first in a series of books that explores how popular culture—magazines, newspapers, theater, and the new industry of moving pictures—portrayed women throughout the twentieth century. It is the story too of how women changed the way the world perceived them.

Chapter One
BIRDS in GILDED CAGES

Newport Society ladies at a garden party, 1905

Women are most beautiful of all——not women sitting on a cloud, idealized, but honest, living, helping actual women——women such as we have here in the United States.

——Charles Gibson, *New York Times*, November 20, 1910

EACH SUMMER,

Boston and New York City's wealthiest families descended upon the coastal town of Newport, Rhode Island. They brought golf clubs, fishing tackle, cats, dogs, and caged canaries. The "ladies"—a term of respect applied to these wealthy well-bred women—brought wardrobes of gowns, dancing slippers, hats, handbags, corsets, and petticoats. They called themselves cottagers. Their summer homes along Bellevue Avenue and Ocean Drive, however, weren't cottages at all. They were marble mansions with dozens of rooms. In these rooms, as many as thirty to sixty servants polished the wood, swept the carpets, shined the silver, and chilled the champagne.

The media referred to American millionaire families—the Astors, the Vanderbilts, the Morgans, the Belmonts, and others—as "polite Society." And yes, Society was capitalized then as a proper noun to signify a specific group of people. When Society was in "residence," the newspapers were full of stories about them and their summer pleasures: horse racing, tennis, fox hunting, lavish dinners, and even more lavish balls. American wealthy families summered in other seaside resorts, such as New York State's Adirondack

Mountains or in Asheville, North Carolina. Newport, however, was "the unrivalled playground of fashion."

A SUMMER DAY IN THE LIFE OF A SOCIETY LADY

A typical turn-of-the-century summer day in Newport for a Society lady might include the following: Breakfast in bed served on a silver tray with a small bouquet of violets. A lazy hour followed, while the lady read the newspaper or her mail and wrote social notes to her acquaintances. Or the lady might dress to ride sidesaddle through the fields on one

The Vanderbilt home, known as the Breakers, was built in Newport, Rhode Island, in 1893 to replace the family's wood house, which had burned the previous year. Several well-known architects as well as artisans and craftspeople from around the world worked on the seventy-room Italian Renaissance–style stone mansion.

of her horses. Then came luncheon. She might dine on the cottage piazza, or the porch. Or she might prefer to ferry out to a friend's yacht moored in the harbor.

After lunch a favorite afternoon ritual for the ladies was parading along Ocean Drive. In the late 1890s, the ladies rode in horse-drawn carriages. They sat as in a showcase, wrote social historian Lloyd Morris, "prepared to be looked at, waiting to be admired in their lacy dresses and feathery hats." And looked at they were—at least by one another. A fashionable lady took particular notice of what other women were wearing or with whom they were socializing. In the early twentieth century, motorcars began replacing horse-drawn vehicles. But the ritual of dressing and parading to be seen and admired did not change. What one lady had, the other soon desired. "I [wish] I had one of those new little electric automobiles," wrote a fashionable lady in her diary in 1901. "The women at Newport have them, and I shall begin to drop hints about it into Papa's mind in a month or so."

This drawing by T. De Thulstrup shows Newport's Bellevue Avenue around the turn of the century. From atop a fine horse-drawn carriage, the ladies of polite Society show off their finery.

Bathing, too, was a simple pleasure as well as another opportunity to be seen. Bathing, however, was not washing in a tub. Bathing meant swimming. But even swimming had a slightly different connotation at the turn of the nineteenth century. A lady floated in the water rather than propelling herself with powerful arm strokes and leg kicks. Her flannel bathing

dress, modestly covering most of her body, would have made such athletic movements quite difficult. The blouse covered her arms, and the skirt fell to just below her knees. Her legs were not bare. She wore flannel stockings and bathing slippers. The Society girl "swims as naturally as she dances," commented the *New York Times*. "She must undergo the scrutiny of the crowd of lookers-on quite as much as when she floats across the ballroom floor."

Dinner usually began at eight thirty in the evening and frequently lasted three hours. Polite Society rarely dined at home—at least not alone. One was invited to dine at another's cottage. Mrs. Ogden Mills could serve dinner for one hundred in her dining room. Seven-course meals were typical. Such a meal might have included oysters, turtle soup, sweet cheeses, fruit, soft clams, a rack of lamb, a fish called terrapin, and canvasback (a wild duck). After dinner came bridge, a card game during which Society couples might gamble hundreds of dollars. A spirited game might continue past midnight.

A more formal night might include a ball beginning at ten in the evening with dinner served at midnight. The parents and grandparents retired at one in the morning, but the younger generation danced until daybreak. The popularity of a hostess often rested on the favors she presented throughout the evening to her guests. Sometimes the favors were simple corsages. More often, especially in the early twentieth century, the favors were expensive fans, enameled watches, or stickpins adorned with real jewels. The hostess distributed the favors to coincide with particular dances. Servants often entered the ballroom with the treasures, or

Members of polite Society considered it their obligation to raise funds for charity. The Vanderbilt estate (above) *was often the setting for charity bazaars and other events.*

remembrances, on trays, or they might be arranged elegantly on a table. The male guest took one of the favors and presented it to his dance partner. The female guest also presented a favor to her dance partner. The favors could be quite expensive, but according to *Harper's Bazaar*, the novelty and quality of the favors—not the food or the music—could determine whether the evening had been a success or failure.

When they finally tired of dancing, the young people moved into the large dining halls for a breakfast of ham, eggs, and coffee. A formal ball might cost tens of thousands of dollars. Attending these balls was expensive too, for a fashionable woman simply couldn't wear the same ball gown more than once in a season.

Men earned the money to make these extravagant summer cottages and cotillion balls possible. But women ruled polite Society. They planned the festivities. They determined who could and could not enter their social orbit. In addition to wealth, property, servants, and a fashionable wardrobe, one other requirement was necessary for membership to Society: notable ancestors. It wasn't good enough to be merely a millionaire or even a billionaire. It was far better to have been born to money than to have earned it.

Society ladies were the turn of the century's media celebrities. Newspaper society columns reported daily on the ladies who moved in and out of this whirlwind of Society. "Miss Post, who was the first lady to automobile alone, has . . . caused many of the ladies of the smart set to take up automobiling," a social reporter wrote. Just making an appearance in Society was often reason enough to be mentioned in the newspaper, as in this news clip: "Austin Gray and Miss Alice

> In addition to wealth, property, servants, and a fashionable wardrobe, one other requirement was necessary for membership to Society: notable ancestors.

Two of Newport's Society women have an outing in what was the equivalent of a sports car in the early 1900s. Compare it to the more sedate black Model-T sedan in the background.

Burham of Boston, whose engagement was announced this week, appeared on Bellevue Avenue this evening, and were congratulated by a large number of cottagers."

Other people vacationed in Newport, to be sure. "Well-to-do" families were those who owned smaller properties. While the father or husband worked, the families had enough money and time for leisure activities. These well-to-do families owned smaller homes, where they might vacation for perhaps a few weeks or a month. The less well-off might rent a hotel room or small home

for a week, while the working class might travel by train to the seacoast for a day trip. Polite Society referred to these other masses of people as the hoi polloi. The hoi polloi, which is Greek for "the many," were simply "everybody else."

The other ten months of the year, Newport was a quiet seacoast town. How did the hoi polloi who lived year-round in Newport feel about their wealthy summer residents? Many resented them and their public displays of wealth. Elizabeth Drexel Lehr wrote that the townspeople "despised the 'cottagers,' and would often

Society had its own beach at Newport (left). At upper right, note the individual cabanas where swimmers could change into their bathing costumes. The hoi polloi went to a public beach where commoners could enjoy themselves. The photograph below shows a group of marines with three women in bathing costumes.

charge the idly rich very high prices and say, Why not?" The local newspaper, in contrast to the *New York Times* society column, editorialized about the cottagers. Their summer season created business for the townspeople. And yet the *Newport Mercury* stated that "the greatest calamity which has ever befallen Newport is making it a fashionable resort in the summer." The calamity wasn't a disaster like a

hurricane. But like a hurricane, polite Society rolled into the quiet seacoast town. They crowded the streets. They claimed the best beach for themselves. They hunted fox through the fields on horseback. And they mostly ignored the hoi polloi who called Newport home all year-round.

Once the season ended, after Labor Day in September, polite Society packed its trunks and returned to the cities. The mansions stood quiet and dark, shuttered for the winter. The hoi polloi of Newport had their tree-lined streets and shops, their wharves, their waves, and their foxes and fields to themselves once again.

WOMEN MAKE NEWS: POLITE SOCIETY AND THE HOI POLLOI, 1904

The July 19, 1904, edition of the *New York Times* printed two stories, one below the other. The first story had this headline: "Newport Society at Vanderbilt Dance." The newspaper reported, "Mrs. Alfred G. Vanderbilt gave the largest dinner of the season." The article included a description of the fairytalelike atmosphere that greeted the guests as they arrived: Potted palms festooned with hundreds of twinkling electric lights lined the driveway. Tall hydrangeas in full purple bloom and vases of long-stemmed red roses were everywhere. "A life-sized portrait of Mrs. Vanderbilt hung over the fireplace framed with white jasmine, her favorite flower," the article stated.

Immediately below that article was the headline for the second story: "Mrs. McMemomin Hurt?" The story began, "Yesterday was washday in the household of Mrs. Annie McMemomin." While hanging out her wash from her third-floor tenement (slum) apartment in New York City, the woman lost her balance and toppled out the open window. She fell to the small yard below, shared by all the families in the tenement. Neighbors ran for a local surgeon, believing McMemomin surely had broken her arms and legs. When the surgeon arrived, however, the woman was back upstairs in her apartment. The doctor was astonished, the newspaper reported. "Aren't you hurt?" he asked.

"Hurt? Go on, it just jarred me, that's all," she answered through "a mouthful of hairpins." Apparently the fall had knocked the hairpins from her hair. She twisted up her hair and then returned to her washtub.

The tone of the stories differed. Mrs. Vanderbilt would be furious if a Society reporter ever described her with a mouthful of hairpins. A reporter wouldn't dare!

Did Alva Vanderbilt read about her dinner party in the newspaper? Perhaps, but quite likely, she did not read about Annie McMemomin's fall. The stories have little in common, one written with awe about a fashionable lady and the other with a bit of amusement about a working-class woman. But they provide a glimpse into the lifestyles of two women from two different social classes on the same summer day.

The Canary in the Cage

During a party one evening, composer Harry Von Tilzer sang one of his new songs. It was a ballad and told a story. Through a ballroom passes a most beautiful woman, the ballad goes. She seems happy, but she isn't. She has married an older man for his wealth and not because she loved him. Although she "lives in a mansion grand," she has wasted her life. She has sold her beauty "for an old man's gold." In the second verse, beauty dies. Her life has been meaningless. "She is only a bird in a gilded cage," sang Harry Von Tilzer.

When he had finished singing, Von Tilzer realized that a few young women in the room were crying. Arthur Lamb, the lyricist, had intended the song to be sentimental, and it seemed he had succeeded. "A Bird in a Gilded Cage" was one the most popular parlor songs of 1900. Parlor songs were popular music meant to be played in the home, usually on a piano. "A Bird in a Gilded Cage" was about a fashionable lady in Society, but the sheet music became a best seller among middle-class and working-class Americans. What did the song mean? The image of a bird in a gilded, or expensive gold-covered, cage was familiar to Americans at the turn of the last century. A canary was a popular parlor pet. Families kept these small yellow birds in cages and enjoyed their cheerful chirping. The bird was fed, watered, petted, and perhaps spoken to, but the bird did not fly. At night a cloth draped over the cage silenced the canary's voice.

Popular songs such as "A Bird in a Gilded Cage" spoke to the limits of women's lives in the early 1900s. Fashions also restricted women. The elegant woman pictured on the cover of this sheet music, for example, is hobbled by her long, tight skirt. Her Merry Widow hat, high collar, and ermine fur muff also limit her ability to move freely and easily.

Fashionable ladies at the turn of the century were very much like birds in gilded cages. The wealthy American man lavished a great deal of money on his wife. He did so, perhaps, because he didn't know what else to do with the money—or with her. He did not share her interests in cotillions and tea parties. Nor did he wish to admit her to his world of business and politics. If she wished to purchase expensive clothes or give jeweled stickpins to her dinner guests, he didn't much care. The woman's sphere was the home. As long as she remained there, he was content.

The lady of polite Society was an ornament. "She was an emblem of some man's power to waste, a measure of his competitive superiority over other men," wrote historian Lloyd Morris. She was the pet canary. The cage was her mansion as well as the admiration of Society. When a man draped the dark cover on the cage, he expected the woman to be silent. He preferred that she did not voice her opinion about issues that he considered men's concerns—business and politics, for example.

What Every Girl Should Know

Elizabeth Meriwether Gilmer followed the social expectations for young women of the times. She got married. Soon after, however, her husband showed the first signs of suffering from a mental illness. He could not hold a job, and his moodiness made him a social outcast. Society frowned upon divorce. Society also did not look favorably on women who worked outside the home. Even so, Elizabeth Gilmer realized she had to earn a living somehow. She began writing newspaper stories. The owner of the *New Orleans Picayune* purchased one of Gilmer's stories for three dollars and offered her a job. The editor of the newspaper, Nathaniel Burbank, wasn't very happy that his new writer was a woman instead of a man. Elizabeth Gilmer, however, proved that she had talent. She also had ambition. She adopted a pen name—Dorothy Dix. Each week her column Sunday Salad appeared on the woman's page of the newspaper.

Sunday Salad was an advice column for the lovelorn, those people who were unlucky in relationships. The column became quite popular. The newspaper doubled her weekly salary and changed the column's title to Dorothy Dix Speaks.

To the question, what is love? she wrote: "Love means caring for someone more than yourself. It is putting somebody else's pleasure and happiness and well-being above your own. It is sacrificing yourself for another and enjoying doing it." While she

believed love was grand, she often cautioned her readers, many of whom were men, to take their time before entering marriage. "Watch your step, boys, and go slow," she advised.

Dorothy Dix did not write about the physical act of lovemaking. Discussions of female sexuality and sexual intercourse were rarely discussed among husbands and wives or even mothers and their daughters. Elsie Clews Parsons held a PhD in sociology and taught courses on family life at Barnard College in New York City. She wrote about female sexuality at a time when few people did. In 1906 she compiled her lectures into a book titled *The Family*. Like Dorothy Dix, Parsons cautioned young people to move slowly into marriage and to delay having children. She was herself happily married and a mother. She believed in monogamy—that is, husbands and wives remaining faithful to one another. But she understood too that many marriages were failures. Society could not condemn divorce without first asking why marriages failed, she wrote. Neither should Society condemn prostitution without questioning why it existed. Perhaps the most shocking passage in the book was Parsons's concept of a "trial marriage." Before taking their marriage vows, a man and woman might engage in sexual activity to determine if they were indeed compatible. If they were not, then they could avoid a troubled marriage and divorce.

Critics called her book "disgusting." Religious leaders denounced her during church services. Newspapers, too, attacked her, questioning how a decent woman could possibly write such a thing. Parsons had proposed that humans adopt "the morality of the barnyard," stated the *New York Herald*. "The idea of men and women living like animals,

Eleven years of unhappy marriage led Elizabeth Meriwether Gilmer (1861–1951) to a nervous breakdown. After leaving her husband and returning home to New Orleans, Louisiana, she turned herself into Dorothy Dix, the nation's highest-paid and most widely read female journalist.

separating at will and contracting new alliances . . . is barbarism and nothing else," stated the *New York Daily Tribune*.

Just because Society didn't approve of premarital sexual relations or divorce does not mean these acts didn't occur. They did. To write about such basic human relationships, however, was to risk breaking the law. The 1873 Comstock Law was named after Anthony Comstock, a former U.S. postal inspector who created the New York Society for the Suppression of Vice. Comstock had championed the law that prohibited the distribution of "obscene, lewd or lascivious" materials through the mail. This objectionable material included information about birth control methods and contraceptive devices.

Margaret Sanger was a nurse. Like Elsie Clews Parsons, Sanger challenged the country's Comstock Law. She began first by speaking in public about health and hygiene. Women in the audience asked her for specific information on how to prevent a pregnancy. Sanger told them what she knew. A condom could prevent conception, and it was a man's responsibility to wear one. There was no contraceptive for women. They questioned her about venereal diseases, which are transmitted through sexual contact. Soon she began writing a newspaper column on health, addressing

Elsie Clews Parsons was an anthropologist, feminist, and pacifist. Her work fell into two areas—sociological studies with a special interest in the politics of sex and gender, and folklore and ethnic writings by the Native Americans of the Southwest. Because one of her studies discussed trial marriage, preachers spoke out against her from their pulpits, newspapers denounced her, and her name was dropped from the Social Register.

these issues. What Every Girl Should Know was the name of her column.

On a Sunday morning when her column on venereal disease was scheduled to appear, Sanger opened the paper and discovered her words simply weren't there. A blank space two columns wide held these words instead: "What every girl should know—Nothing. By order of the Post-Office Department." "The words *gonorrhea* and *syphilis* had appeared in that article, and Anthony Comstock . . . did not like them," said Sanger.

Sanger would not be so easily silenced, however. As a nurse in tenement buildings on New York's Lower East Side, she had nursed families who could not afford food and clothing for their children. Worse, she had nursed women who had attempted to end unwanted pregnancies the only way they knew—through dangerous abortions or attempts at abortions. She listened to a doctor advise a woman to turn her husband out of their bed. He could sleep on the fire escape or the tenement roof, if necessary, for another pregnancy would surely kill her. The doctor was sympathetic, but the Comstock Law prevented him from telling her how to have sexual relations without becoming pregnant. Within a short time, the woman became pregnant again and died.

The death of that woman—her name was Sadie—helped Margaret Sanger make up her mind. She would devote her life's work to educating women about contraception. Before she could teach women how to prevent pregnancy, however, she first had to learn about the biology of conception. She traveled to Europe with her

> On a Sunday morning when her column on venereal disease was scheduled to appear, Sanger opened the paper and discovered her words simply weren't there. A blank space two columns wide held these words instead: "What every girl should know—Nothing. By order of the Post-Office Department."
>
> —Margaret Sanger, *An Autobiography*, 1938

Margaret Sanger's experience made her aware of the social injustices of birth control. While working as a midwife in New York City's poorest neighborhoods, she saw women drained of their health by too many pregnancies. Wealthy women, however, had access to birth control information and could afford imported products such as condoms or spermicides. Sanger is shown here in 1908 with the younger of her two sons.

husband and children. France was more open about sexual matters. French mothers passed their knowledge on to their daughters, and they told Margaret Sanger what they knew. When she returned to the United States, she would endure ridicule and imprisonment to help women understand the biology of their bodies.

THE GIBSON GIRL MYSTERY

Publishers had been printing magazines for most of the nineteenth century. At the turn of the century, however, magazines became one of the United States' first mass-marketed media. Many had a circulation (or readership) of more than one hundred thousand copies. By 1905 approximately six thousand mass-marketed magazines were available on newsstands. The most popular women's magazine was *Ladies' Home Journal*. The magazine's circulation was an impressive one million readers. By 1919 the readership would soar to two million.

Women's magazines featured articles and short stories that the editors believed were of interest to women. *Ladies' Home Journal*, for example, published an article by President Theodore Roosevelt on the sacredness of motherhood, a profile of actress Sarah Bernhardt, and homemaking tips, such as "Twenty-Six Ways to Serve Eggs" (deviled, steamed, scalloped, diced into egg salad, or whipped into any number of omelets, just to name a few). Humor, too, was a feature of many magazines. Cartoons and short anecdotes punctuated the pages, and women were often the subject of the jest. One story from a 1907 *Ladies' Home Journal* makes fun of the Society lady's dependence on her servants to keep the household running smoothly. In the story,

the cook's absence leads the young mistress of the house to offer to help the maid prepare the Sunday luncheon. The flurried maid, who had been struggling in the kitchen with a coffee machine that refused to work, confessed that she had forgotten to wash the lettuce. "Well, never mind, Eliza. Go on with the coffee, and I'll do it," said the considerate mistress. "Where do you keep the soap?"

Stories such as these were more than humorous. They reflected attitudes about the wealthy and, in doing so, suggested stereotypes about women's roles in the home. The magazine's visual images, too, suggested how a woman might dress and behave. Fashion articles had pages of illustrations. A person who wore the latest fashions showcased in these magazines was called a fashion plate. The term relates to the publishing practice of using hand-colored engravings to create the fashion illustration.

CALLING WOMEN "GIRLS"

Classic illustrations of women in the magazines of the early 1900s were images of "girls"—the Gibson girl, the Christy girl, the Brinkley girl. However, when illustrator Charles Gibson drew a male figure, the media called him the Gibson man and never the Gibson boy.

The practice of calling grown women "girls" was common at the turn of the century, especially in the workplace. The Hello girls operated telephone switchboards. Those who worked in department stores were shopgirls. "Girl stenographers" worked in offices. To be fair, young men who worked in offices were called office boys. But they were young and inexperienced men just entering the workforce. As they advanced in their responsibilities, they became businessmen. Women, however, no matter their age, more often than not remained "girls."

The use of "girl" to refer to grown women is disprespectful. A girl is a child, someone not fully grown or able to take care of herself. The word also suggests a lower class of working woman, someone who has to work for a living rather than someone who chooses a career in a profession, such as business or law.

The Gibson girl represented the feminine ideal at the turn of the last century. She was beautiful and regal—perhaps even a bit arrogant—but she also seemed to give off an air of confidence and competence. And most subtle of all, she seemed to have a sense of humor about the world and about herself.

The woman who appeared most frequently on the cover of these increasingly popular magazines was the Gibson girl. Her image was unlike those of American women that had appeared in the nineteenth century. Physically, she looked different. She was tall, with an incredibly tiny waist. She wore her hair swept up into a softly twisted bun called a chignon, revealing her long, swanlike neck. What distinguished her more than any physical characteristics, however, was her attitude. Images of women in the nineteenth century had frequently portrayed them as gentle, nurturing, and virtuous. These images also often depicted women in a home environment—playing the piano, sewing, caring for the ill, or reading a prayer book. The lift of the Gibson girl's chin and her half-closed eyes, however, suggested that she was more aloof then nurturing. Some thought her sophisticated. Others thought her haughty or conceited. She didn't stay at home, either. The images placed her on a golf course or on the beach. The media quickly labeled her "the typical American girl."

The artist who created this image was Charles Dana Gibson. The Gibson girl appeared on the covers of many popular magazines, including *Collier's Weekly, Ladies' Home Journal,* and *McClure's.* Many of the illustrations suggested a story as well as an attitude. The story, however, was often a satirical comment on polite Society. In one image, the girl wears a wedding gown. Beside her stands the groom. He is short, old, and balding. The image echoes the lyrics of "A Bird in a Gilded Cage."

In other images, the man is the one who is trapped by the Gibson girl's beauty and changing emotions. In a drawing titled "The Weaker Sex," for example, four Gibson girls lean over a table. One holds a magnifying glass and a knitting needle. On the table, under the glass, is a miniature man. He is on his knees as if begging. The girls are apparently examining him while also sticking him with the needle. The drawing's title is ironic. Turn-of-the-century attitudes regarded women as the weaker sex, not men. Perhaps Gibson was suggesting that the stereotype was false. Did women only pretend to be weaker in order to control men?

Another illustration called "Summer Sports" showed Gibson girls flying kites. Looking more closely, the viewer sees that the kites are again miniature men. Was Gibson suggesting that women toyed with men's hearts and money just for the sport of it? Part of the appeal of the Gibson girl was debating just what

This illustration by Charles Dana Gibson is ironically titled "The Weaker Sex." Dating to about 1903, it shows Gibson girls holding the advantage over a tiny man, whom they are prodding with a knitting needle.

each illustration meant. Over the years, the Gibson girl golfed daringly and kissed a young man (known as the Gibson man) on a beach that looked very similar to the one in Newport. She eventually married and became a mother. In some drawings, she was a widow.

The Gibson girl became a media sensation. Suddenly, the girl's image appeared on china, silverware, and satin pillows. Real American girls twisted their hair into chignons and wore Gibson girl skirts and shirtwaists with stiff, high-necked collars. Who was the Gibson girl really? Was she fact, or was she fancy? Americans wanted to know. Some said she was a Society lady, one who summered at Newport. Or she was perhaps a southern belle. No, said others, she was President Theodore Roosevelt's beautiful teenage daughter Alice, who rode bicycles without a chaperone and smoked cigarettes in public. No, no! said those of the working class. She was one of the hoi polloi, a poor immigrant Irish girl who worked as a maid and earned a few precious pennies by modeling for Charles Gibson in his studio. Every class of woman, it seemed, saw (or wanted to see) themselves in Gibson's images.

In 1905 reporter William Griffith interviewed Charles Gibson in his studio. Gibson's secretary soon interrupted the interview. The models had arrived, she told

The 1915 portrait at left shows each of three young women wearing Gibson girl hairstyles. The one at right shows a woman in Gibson-style clothing—even while fishing. Magazine illustrators had a major influence on fashion trends in the first two decades of the twentieth century and none more so than Charles Dana Gibson.

the artist. If the reporter thought he'd meet the real Gibson girl and solve the mystery at last, he was disappointed. "A bevy [group] of fair and forty models" entered the studio. Each was a "golden girl," the author wrote, but Charles Gibson turned every one away. None was quite right for the drawing he had in mind. "Among the hundreds of models who come, it is only occasionally that a suitable one materializes," Gibson explained.

In a later interview, Gibson spoke about how he came to draw his famous cultural icon. "I never consciously sat to work to create a specific type of the American girl," Gibson told the reporter. "I saw her on the streets, I saw her at the theatres, I saw her in the churches, I saw her everywhere and doing everything." She was, he said, a working girl in a department store. She was a Society lady promenading (walking) on New York City's Fifth Avenue. He had gotten his inspiration, he said, from tens of thousands of American women.

Gibson's image of the American girl had become so real that many didn't want to believe she was one artist's idea of womanhood. They wanted her to be real. But ideals and images also change with the times. After 1910 the Gibson girl appeared less frequently in magazine illustrations. Others were taking her place. They, too, got their names from their artist creators: Harrison Fisher, Howard Chandler Christy, and Nell Brinkley.

Many models posed as Gibson girls, but perhaps the most famous was the Belgian-born actress, Camille Clifford. This 1900 photograph highlights the Gibson-inspired S-curve silhouette—achieved by using a swan-bill corset.

The Fisher, Christy, and Brinkley Girls

The Fisher girl was younger than the Gibson girl, more innocent and less sophisticated. Harrison Fisher created a little rhyme about his artistic creation:

> She is gentle, she is shy;
> But there's mischief in her eye.
> She's a flirt.

The Fisher girl was also "outdoorsy." She canoed, she rode horses, and she played tennis. The Christy girl, too, was often portrayed as a sports-minded college student. Both the Fisher and the Christy girls were smart and physically fit. Most images show them outside rather than inside the home. They weren't locked in a cage.

The images of American "girls" on magazines reflected a real-world change in women's roles. More young women were going to college. The great majority of women, however, did not. Even so, many young, unmarried women left the home to work in offices as secretaries, telephone operators, or typists; in schools as teachers; and in hospitals as nurses. Some women were artists. Jessie Willcox Smith and Elizabeth Shippen Green attended Philadelphia's Drexel Institute of Art, Science, and Industry. The works of both women focused on children. Willcox's images appeared in hundreds of magazines, including *Good Housekeeping* and *Collier's Weekly*. In later years, she created advertising images for such products as Campbell's soup and Ivory soap, which featured healthy, happy children.

Harrison Fisher (1875–1934) drew beautiful young women such as the one above. The large number of cover illustrations he did for major magazines earned him the nickname the Father of a Thousand Girls.

Is College Dangerous to a Woman's Health?

As a young girl growing up in the second half of the nineteenth century, Martha Carey Thomas yearned to go to college. She had never before met a college woman, and the first time she did so, she was timid, even afraid. College women were an anomaly, rare and quite possibly not normal female beings. Thomas knew well the work of Dr. Edward Clarke, a medical doctor and professor of medicine at Harvard University in Massachusetts. In a book published in the 1870s, Clarke stated that a woman could indeed study and master the same college subjects that a man studied. But in doing so, the woman would ruin her health. Concentration on college work would damage her reproductive organs, the doctor claimed. Thinking drained energy from a woman's ovaries and led to hysteria and "other derangements of the nervous system." An especially dangerous time for women occurred during her monthly menstruation, many physicians of the nineteenth century believed. Clarke suggested that women should be excused from all studies during her period.

Martha Carey Thomas feared that perhaps Clarke was right. But she desired a college education, no matter the physical risks. In 1873 she enrolled at Cornell University in New York. Before she did so, however, she visited a woman who had graduated from New York's Vassar College.

Martha Carey Thomas, who preferred to be known as Carey Thomas, was a strong supporter of women's rights. With several of her female friends, she gave a large amount of money to the Johns Hopkins University Medical School in Maryland. In accepting the gift, the school agreed to admit women to the school on an equal basis with men.

Thomas was a bit nervous about the meeting, fearing this unusual creature might have "hoofs and horns." To her surprise, however, the college-educated woman wasn't abnormal at all. Nor was she an invalid. She was, in fact, tall and rather attractive, Thomas stated.

After graduating from Cornell, Martha Carey Thomas enrolled for postgraduate studies at the University of Leipzig in Germany. However, once there, she found that the university would not award a PhD to a woman. Worse yet, she was forced to sit behind a screen during classes so that the male students would not be distracted by her presence. She transferred to the University of Zurich in Switzerland from which she graduated at the top of her class.

By 1900 Thomas had become the president of Bryn Mawr College in Pennsylvania, a school for women. Both her reproductive organs and her nervous system were unharmed by her studies or her career in education. She began writing essays encouraging other women to enroll in college. She also encouraged colleges to create meaningful and challenging courses of study for women students.

"Now women who have been to college are as plentiful as blackberries on summer hedges," Thomas wrote in 1908. In comparison to when she was a girl, it must have seemed so. In actuality, in 1900 only about 2 percent of the nation's young people enrolled in college after high school. Of these college students, approximately 19 percent were women. And most of those women (though not all) were from families considered well-to-do.

Many women attended all-female colleges. Other female students applied to colleges that only men attended. More often than not, they were refused admission. But when they did attend, the women faced discrimination, such as being unable to enter the library when male students were studying.

What did college women study? Some enrolled in art, music, and those homemaking subjects that could prepare them to become knowledgeable wives and mothers. Others, however, wanted very badly to study subjects such as medicine and law. Many colleges refused to admit women into more rigorous academic programs. The old assumption that women simply weren't as clever as men in certain subject areas still existed in the first few decades of the twentieth century.

Howard Chandler Christy's work was published in many books and almost all major magazines in the early years of the twentieth century. The posters above feature the famous Christy girl.

And then there was the Brinkley girl. In 1905, when much of the United States was still puzzling over who the real Gibson girl might be, teenager Nell Brinkley was sketching images of American women, first for the *Denver Post* and later for newspapers owned by publisher William Randolph Hearst.

Hearst wanted romantic rather than realistic images of women, he told his artist. Nell Brinkley gave him what he wanted. Brinkley costumed her wealthy socialite characters in ruffled gowns. Her working girl, however, was more plainly dressed, though still feminine. Sometimes Brinkley drew her in a factory. She drew her on a farm wearing a kerchief and holding a rake. The caption for one of her cartoons read, "Her pretty fingers are dabbled in everything that a man can do—and the fingers are agile and skilled too, my friend." The Brinkley girl might have been feminine and romantic, but she was also independent and at times shockingly daring. "Brinkley's women laugh with their mouths wide open," says historian Trina Robbins. One cartoon showed her riding a surfboard. While the others in the image wear bathing caps, the Brinkley girl's curly hair is loose and free. Unlike the tiny-waisted Gibson girl, she did not need a corset to be attractive. Nor did she need a man to be happy.

Nell Brinkley, too, was a new kind of woman—what the media was beginning to call the new American woman. She was a suffragist. She believed that women should have the right to vote. "For every twenty romantic panels she supplied [the newspaper]," wrote historian Trina Robbins, "she would do one on the subject of suffrage or working women—or one of her other favorite subjects— women active in sports or the outdoors." In 1915 Brinkley wrote this caption under an illustration of a Brinkley girl enjoying the outdoors: "She tramps the pine woods and the hill in knickerbockers, her waist free of corseting and her limbs of skirts; her pack on her shoulder; and never missing [a] man!"

Nell Brinkley's work was sensitive to the many issues women faced in the early 1900s. The shower of Brinkley girls above is lovely. But it also shows problems that many women faced—housing shortages and landlords reluctant to rent to poor women.

The women on the magazine covers—whether drawn by Gibson, Fisher, Christy, or Brinkley—were always white. Women of color were rarely represented in popular magazines at the turn of the century—neither on the covers nor in the magazine's advertisements. Images of African American women appeared most frequently in the *Crisis*, a publication of the newly formed National Association for the Advancement of Colored People (NAACP). The *Crisis* was a general interest rather than a woman's magazine. Education was a frequent subject. The August 1922 cover photograph showed a young African American woman in a graduation cap and gown.

The "girls" on the covers of women's magazines such as *Ladies' Home Journal* and *Good Housekeeping* were illustrations. As Charles Gibson had said repeatedly, the Gibson girl didn't exist. However, the women's images on the covers of the *Crisis* were photographs. These were real African American women. The difference is important, says Carolyn Kitch, a former editor of *Good Housekeeping*. "Illustration implies ideals," she said. A photograph, however, is more realistic. The photographs of women on the cover of the *Crisis* were "proof" that African American women were also feminine and fashionable. They, too, were changing with the times, going to school, and entering the public sphere.

> The photographs of women on the cover of the *Crisis* were "proof" that African American women were also feminine and fashionable.

UNLATCHING THE CAGE

The century was turning, and life was changing, even within polite Society. It can be lonely living in a cage, even one that glitters, and women were becoming disillusioned with extravagance. Perhaps they simply became bored with one another. They were certainly bored with the gilded cage. "If intelligent [the lady] wanted to be judged on her merits; not on her charms, her caprice [impulsiveness] and her costliness," wrote historian Lloyd Morris. "This was a new desire."

Was it really a new desire? Or was it just that women had found new ways to make their viewpoints known? One means of expression was the woman's club, which women had begun forming in cities across the United States in the late nineteenth century. Initially, the clubwomen met to read and discuss books. Their discussions soon included social welfare and ways to improve their communities.

Many women also became suffragists. Women had been fighting to win the vote since the mid-nineteenth century, so suffrage (the right to vote) wasn't a new issue. What was new, however, were the

ways in which women began expressing this desire. Visual images drawn as editorial cartoons were one of the suffragists' new strategies. Images were powerful. The popularity of the Gibson girl and her sisters Christy, Fisher, and Brinkley proved that. Between 1910 and 1920, writes women's historian Alice Sheppard, dozens of women artists and not just Nell Brinkley "seized their drawing pens, pencils, grease crayons, and brushes to contribute cartoons for suffrage." In one cartoon, Justice (portrayed as a woman in a white flowing robe) pushed men away from the ballot box so that a woman could cast her vote. Cartoonist Laura Foster titled her cartoon, "Justice—Make Way!"

Women in polite Society too were joining the women's suffrage movement. Alva Vanderbilt—who had gotten a divorce and later married O. H. P. Belmont—had become a suffragist. The *New York Times* often reported on Alva Belmont's lavish parties at her Newport mansion. By 1909 the newspaper was reporting on her teas and luncheons for suffragists and her work in planning demonstrations to advance the rights of women. She opened a suffrage headquarters in New York City and established a soup kitchen to provide food for poor women. Eventually, her Marble House in Newport was closed even in summer.

Alva Belmont desired to be more than a bird in a gilded cage. In the years to come, she and many other women like her would

Mrs. Alva Belmont, previously married to William K. Vanderbilt, became an important figure in social and political circles. She became president of the National Woman's Party (NWP) and an active advocate of women's suffrage. The photo shows a 1914 suffrage meeting at her Newport mansion, known as Marble House.

ZITKALA-SA'S STORY

Gertrude Simmons Bonnin is best known by her pen name, Zitkala-Sa. Her autobiographical collection American Indian Stories *tells of the hardships she encountered when placed in one of the several manual labor boarding schools that were designed by the U.S. government to "civilize" Native American children.*

Persons Who Interest Us was a column in *Harper's Bazaar*. In April 1900, one of the people who interested the magazine's editors was Zitkala-Sa. This young "Indian girl," was both beautiful and a talented writer. The editors added, however, that as a child, Zitkala-Sa had been "a veritable little savage, running wild over the prairie and speaking no language but her own."

The language she spoke, Sioux, was the language of her mother. Born Gertrude Simmons in 1876, she was among the first generation of Native American children to grow up on a reservation in South Dakota. Her mother had taught her the traditions of her people. The editors of *Harper's Bazaar* might have thought the Indian girl a savage, but Zitkala-Sa (which means "Red Bird") viewed herself differently. "I was a wild little girl of seven," she wrote. "Loosely clad in a slip of brown buckskin, and light footed with a pair of soft moccasins on my feet, I was as free as the wind that blew my hair. . . ."

To Zitkala-Sa, her wildness meant freedom. It was the joy of being one with nature. "Savage," on the other hand, suggests an altogether different image—a beastly or an uncivilized creature. At the turn of the century, the use of *savage* to describe a Native American woman in a popular magazine reflected a common stereotype many white Americans held about Native Americans. These perceptions were rooted in popular culture of the nineteenth century, including advertisements and Wild West shows that traveled across the country. Some tobacco companies, for example, had created labels for their products using the image of an Indian maiden in a wilderness setting, barefoot and often bare breasted. An advertising picture of partially dressed white women would have been shocking. Yet such images of Native American women appeared frequently.

At the time *Harper's Bazaar* published its profile of the Native American author, Zitkala-Sa was a social reformer, fighting for improved health care and educational opportunities for Native Americans. She wrote essays for popular magazines about her life on the reservation.

succeed in unlatching the cage. "Just remember this," Belmont told the newspaper reporters who continued to follow her everyday activities, "the home is not the only sphere for women by any means."

> "Just remember this, the home is not the only sphere for women by any means."
>
> —Ava Belmont, 1912

Attending college, joining a women's club, or participating in the suffrage movement—these were ways that women could take on leadership roles and express their ideas. But fate, too, presented women with daunting challenges—thrusting women into situations that tested their stamina and nerve. How they responded to these challenges proved that women were indeed more than just birds in gilded cages. One tragic event that tested many women's mettle occurred on the evening of April 14, 1912, in the middle of the Atlantic Ocean.

FORTUNE AND FATE AT SEA

At the turn of the century, Margaret Tobin Brown and her husband, James, had made their fortune in silver mining in Colorado. The Browns' new wealth, however, didn't guarantee them a place in polite Society. The ladies of Newport, Rhode Island, in particular considered Margaret Brown common. One article in the *New York Times* reported that her pearls were imitation—a shocking revelation in polite Society.

In 1912 Brown, like many wealthy people in the United States, had toured Europe with her daughter. After receiving a telegram of a family emergency at home, she booked passage home on the White Star Line's newest steamship, *Titanic*. Her daughter remained in Paris.

The *Titanic* was indeed titanic, or gigantic. She was the longest, tallest ship in the world and the most luxurious. The six-day voyage across the Atlantic would be *Titanic*'s first. The first-class passengers on *Titanic*'s maiden voyage were an impressive group of prominent

men and women from polite Society, including bankers, merchants, a countess, an artist, and an aide to the president of the United States. The ship also carried second-class passengers, including an African American family. More than seven hundred third-class passengers, including immigrants who spoke little or no English, traveled in steerage. Accommodations were on the lower levels near the ship's rudder and steering mechanisms. The least expensive fare on board, steerage accommodations were basically dormitory-style. Some who paid a little more might have enjoyed a narrow room with space enough for a bunk and a sink but little else. Passengers in steerage were not allowed to mingle with first- or second-class passengers. A gate prevented them from climbing the stairs to the first- and second-class cabins.

Just before midnight on the evening of April 14, *Titanic* collided with an iceberg, tearing a hole in its hull. "Women and children first" had long been the code of the sea. *Titanic*'s crew followed the code, although clearly there were not enough lifeboats to safely load all the passengers. While the ship's musicians played, men kissed their wives farewell and stepped back from the lifeboats. Some women refused to leave their husbands, and some men managed to find room within the boats.

In Great Britain and in the United States, a wireless radio telegram indicated that the *Titanic* had struck an iceberg. "*Titanic* Sunk, No Lives Lost" reported the *Daily Mail* of London just two days after the event. The story was inaccurate. A few agonizing days passed before the survivors who had been rescued by the *Carpathia*, a ship

In May 1912, Mrs. Margaret Brown is shown presenting a trophy award to Captain Arthur Henry Rostron of the Carpathia *for his service in the rescue of the* Titanic. *Brown, too, was worthy of a trophy. Her heroic actions during the disaster were later the basis for a successful Broadway musical and movie,* The Unsinkable Molly Brown.

that happened to be nearby, reached New York City. Slowly, through their eyewitness accounts, the world learned what had happened on the sea that night. More than 1,600 lives had been lost. Only 739 passengers and crew had survived.

The men who went down with the ship were heroes in the eyes of the world. So, too, were many of the women who took charge of the oars and boosted the spirits of those who witnessed the *Titanic* going down. "Women Revealed as Heroines by Wreck" was a headline in the *New York Times* on April 20, 1912. From eyewitness accounts, the reporter stated, "Women were the central figures in the great sea tragedy."

When told to abandon ship, first-class passenger Margaret Brown, the woman who had been ignored by polite Society, dressed in a wool suit, a fur coat, and multiple pairs of wool stockings. She spoke a number of foreign languages and helped many immigrant women find places in a lifeboat. She herself took a seat in boat number six. She shared her coat and wool stockings with other women. Then she gripped the oars and began to pull. She made the others take turns rowing so they would keep warm.

In lifeboat eight, the Countess of Rothes took the oars, as did her maid. Women later testified that the countess had taken the oars when one of the seamen simply could not

row skillfully. The countess was not an athlete or a sportswoman. Nevertheless, one of the crew who was in the lifeboat told reporters, "She was more of a man than any we had in that boat."

In other boats too, the women rowed—women such as "Mrs. Thayer," the wife of the vice president of the Pennsylvania Railroad, and "Mrs. Widener," the wife of a wealthy Philadelphia businessman. Maids and immigrant women, too, took their turns at the oars. There were no class distinctions in the lifeboats, just the will to pull together and survive. First, they pulled away from the sinking ship so as not to be sucked into its whirlpool. Later, they rowed hour after hour in hopes that some ship somewhere had heard *Titanic*'s distress calls. One ship did, the *Carpathia*. As dawn broke, the *Carpathia* appeared on the horizon.

Popular media would later label Margaret Tobin Brown as the Unsinkable Molly Brown because she had survived the tragedy and inspired hope in other women survivors. Brown had always been feisty, but her experience aboard *Titanic* changed her. She would later fight for maritime (sailing) reform and for women's rights. In 1914 she would throw her big-brimmed Society hat into the political ring and run for the U.S. Senate in Colorado. She lost the election, but she never lost her commitment to social justice.

FLASHBACK: THE START OF THE WOMAN'S RIGHTS MOVEMENT

"It's coming sooner than most people think," suffragist Susan B. Anthony stated in 1895, referring to women winning the right to vote. At the time, women had been fighting for enfranchisement (the right to vote) for almost fifty years. Efforts in the nineteenth century had failed to force Congress to pass an amendment to the Constitution giving women the vote. But leaders of the women's suffrage movement weren't about to give up.

In May 1907, the magazine *Woman's Home Companion* published an article by Charlotte Perkins Gilman titled "The Progress of Women in the Last Fifty Years." Who were these strong-willed and equality-minded women? Why were they so determined to win full citizenship for all American women?

In 1848 Elizabeth Cady Stanton and Susan B. Anthony organized the first Woman's Rights Convention. Both women were abolitionists, who opposed slavery and were working to abolish it. They had spoken in front of hostile mobs of white slaveholders. They were convinced that women too were in bondage. During that first conference, held in Seneca Falls, New York, Stanton read her "Declaration of Sentiments." The document presented eighteen areas in which women lacked rights, placing them in bondage to men. These areas included the following:

Because she could not vote, a woman had no voice in the laws that governed her. As a child, she belonged to her father. Once married, she had no right to property. The home in which she lived, the dishes, even her clothing belonged not to her but to her husband. Money she might earn on her own belonged not to her but to her husband. Marriage laws required her to obey her husband. A husband had the legal right to punish his wife if he felt her behavior required it. Should a woman divorce or separate from her husband, he—not she—had legal right to their children. Her education was limited to those fields that man considered proper for a woman. Many schools denied women admittance to study law or medicine. Without equal educational opportunities, a woman could never be fully independent of her father or her husband.

In her article, Gilman wrote that the "declaration of sentiments" showed "plainly and sadly" the status of women in the United States at the time. Politically, woman was helpless. Gilman wrote: "Speaking generally, the woman had not only no voice in the management of the country, but she had no control of her property, earned or inherited; no

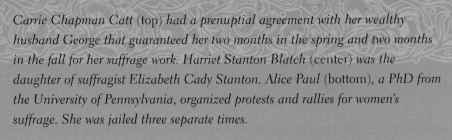

control of her own children; no control even of her own person. If that is not a condition of slavery, it bears a close resemblance to it."

Suffrage was about much more than just voting in a presidential election. It was, as Stanton had expressed it, about basic human rights for women.

By 1907, fifty-eight years after the convention, suffragists had won many battles. Gilman reminded her readers that nine states and the District of Columbia had passed laws giving mothers and fathers equal guardianship of their children. Four states—Wyoming, Colorado, Idaho, and Utah—had given women the right to vote. The suffrage movement was not a failure, Gilman stressed. Three hundred people had attended that first woman's rights convention in 1848. In 1906 membership in women's clubs and suffrage organizations had soared into the millions. It was proof, wrote Gilman, that women were serious about social change.

In the years to come, however, the new leaders of the suffrage movement would not agree on the best strategy of advancing woman's rights. Carrie Chapman Catt belonged to the National American Woman Suffrage Association (NAWSA). Her strategy was to organize and educate, working state by state for the passage of laws favorable to women's rights. Some suffragists, such as Alice Paul and Harriet Stanton Blatch, believed radical new measures were necessary. These measures included demonstrations to call attention to the cause. Alice Paul would picket the White House, chaining herself to the fence, demanding that the president support an amendment to the Constitution supporting women's suffrage. Arrested, she went on a hunger strike and was force fed by doctors. Eventually, Paul and her followers broke away from the NAWSA and formed the more radical National Woman's Party.

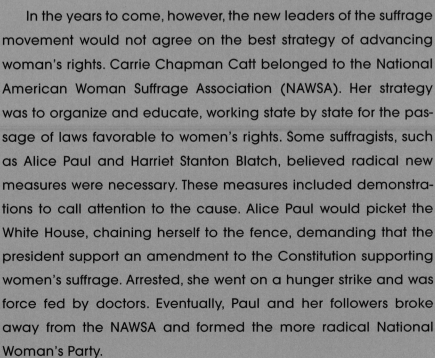

fashions, fitness, and fastidious women

Ladies try on the latest 1910 styles in a dress salon.

"*Certainly the shops are visions of beauty* and if there is a woman who does not delight in visiting them, she is to be pitied for she is losing one of a woman's legitimate pleasures in life."

—"Women Here and There—Her Frills and Fancies," *New York Times*, September 23, 1900

a fastidious woman was fussy and hard to please.

At the turn of the century, being fastidious in one's choice of clothing was apparently a good thing, according to an advertisement for Abercrombie & Fitch Company. The company confidently announced that it could outfit a fastidious woman for any outdoor activity.

Women in polite Society were not the only fastidious women when it came to fashion. Women in other social classes also kept a keen eye on fashion trends as reported in newspapers or magazines. Some women, such as farm women, studied the pages of the Sears® catalog for fashion ideas. A male farmer in Michigan complained in a letter that "farm women, as well, are slaves to fashion." Another farmer also complained that in his home, all his money seemed to go toward keeping his daughters "dressed to keep up with so-called society." What these men and others like them might not have realized, however, is that fashion wasn't quite as whimsical as it appeared to be, nor was it about the wealth of a woman's husband or father.

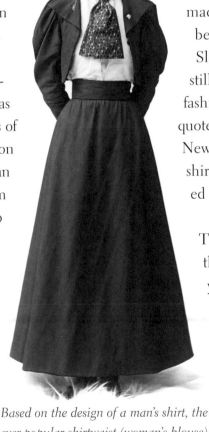

Based on the design of a man's shirt, the ever-popular shirtwaist (woman's blouse) was first worn in the early 1900s. The schoolteacher in this 1905 photograph was up-to-date with the addition of an ascot (scarf) to her costume.

Clothing communicated a woman's confidence and self-esteem. Fashion also reflected women's changing roles in society.

"The shirtwaist [blouse] will be with us more than ever this summer," predicted the *Indianapolis Journal* on New Year's Day, 1900. "Women are wearing shirtwaists because they are comfortable, because they can be made to fit any form, and because they are mannish. Sleeves will be smaller, but still not tight." In making this fashion forecast, the newspaper quoted a dry goods salesman from New York City, A. P. Hurst. "The shirtwaist is here to stay," he stated confidently.

Hurst was mostly correct. The shirtwaist was in vogue at the turn of the century. And yes, the shirtwaist was similar to a man's shirt. It had a stiff, high-necked collar and buttons down the front. Women often wore one with a floppy bow or tie. Some pinned a brooch to the collar. But Hurst was wrong to assume that any fashion would remain in vogue forever.

The length of a woman's skirt, for example, was already shrinking 1 or 2 inches (2 to 5 centimeters) by 1900. The skirt no longer swept the ground, and women dared to show a bit of ankle. Even though that ankle was never bare (at least not in public), this was a rather shocking fashion development. Even so, many women must have welcomed the fashion change. Skirts that had swept the often muddy and icy streets soon became filthy and frayed.

As women's physical and social activities changed, so too did women's fashions. In the 1880s, playing lawn tennis was one of the few acceptable outdoor activities for women. On the court, the fastidious female player held up her voluminous skirt and petticoats in one hand. In her other hand, she held her racket. Somehow she managed to pop the ball back over the net without tripping on the yards of material that swathed her legs. By the 1890s, women's physical activities were changing. An advertisement for Overman Wheel Company, makers of Victor bicycles, described the change this way:

THE TRAILING SKIRT — DEATH LOVES A SHINING MARK.

In this drawing from 1900, Samuel Ehrhart pokes fun at fashion, specifically the dangers of germs collected by skirts dragging on the ground. Amidst the dust the maid is brushing from her mistress's gown are letters spelling out typhoid fever, consumption, influenza, and other dreaded diseases of the time.

The <u>Spinning</u> Wheels of day gone by
Give way to Spinning <u>wheels</u> that fly.
And damsels fair do lightly tread
The graceful VICTOR now, instead.

Once ladies began "spinning" about town, those long skirts had to go. Skirts often became tangled in greasy sprockets and spokes. Wearing slightly shorter skirts was one solution. Wearing a skirt with leggings or trousers underneath was

ACTRESSES AS BICYCLE RIDERS.

The length of women's skirts gradually changed in the early 1900s as bicycling outfits became popular. The image above shows the latest "short" skirts being modeled by actresses, at least two of whom were well known at the time. Anna Held is shown at the top right and Lillian Russell at bottom right.

another. That way, a lady could hike her skirt a little bit without revealing her bare legs. Some women wore a "bicycle suit." This was a split skirt that a woman wore with high-top boots. The spinning wheels of the bicycle soon gave way to the churning wheels of the motorcar. "When women began to move their feet about the pedals of a car," wrote journalist Mark Sullivan in 1926, "long skirts became an inconvenience."

In college, women began to exercise on gymnasium equipment and even to play basketball. High buttoned boots and stiff collars with floppy bow ties wouldn't do. Other physical activities also had designers ripping out seams and redesigning styles. The turkey trot, the grizzly bear, the bunny hug, and other "animal dances" became wildly popular in the 1910s. A young woman needed more wiggle room than a stiff-boned corset could provide.

The Outdoor Girls of Deepdale

The Outdoor Girls was a series of popular books published from 1913 through 1933. Each book featured the same four female characters: Betty Nelson, Grace Ford, Amy Stonington, and Mollie Billette. The following scene comes from the opening pages of the first book in the series, *The Outdoor Girls of Deepdale.*

The four girls are walking down Main Street, two by two. Their arms encircle one another's waists. They chatter and giggle. It was the last day of classes at Deepdale High School. To celebrate their summer vacation, the girls decide to treat themselves to ice-cream sodas in Pierson's Drugstore.

Women Make News: Alice Ramsey's Coast-to-Coast Endurance Record, 1909

"Good driving has nothing to do with sex. It's all above the collar," said Alice Ramsey. In addition to requiring clear thinking and good judgment, operating an automobile in the first two decades of the twentieth century required stamina and physical strength. It also demanded intelligence, especially if the driver was attempting to drive approximately 3,993 miles (6,429 kilometers) from New York City to Sacramento, California. At the time, road maps weren't available because there weren't even roads in some parts of the country! And the established routes for horse-drawn vehicles wouldn't work, because a horse can swim across a river, but an automobile can't.

Alice Ramsey was twenty-one years old and a housewife when she first began driving. She participated in two driving endurance races in 1908. A year later, a sales manager for the Maxwell-Briscoe Company proposed that she attempt to drive one of the company's touring cars coast-to-coast. The journey was a publicity stunt. The manufacturer of Maxwell motorcars hoped it would excite Americans and convince them not only that cars were here to stay but also that Maxwell cars were safe and reliable.

"I was flabbergasted at the proposition," Ramsey said. But she accepted. The *New York Times* was equally amazed. "Unassisted she will have to pick the route, guide the car across the Rocky Mountains, and, in fact, will travel over roads and routes that would tax an expert male driver, yet alone she will do all this and with confidence, too, of reaching the Pacific Coast without trouble by July 16."

Ramsey had three traveling companions with her—all women. None of the three could drive. The responsibility for navigating the Maxwell across the United States rested solely with Ramsey. So did the automobile repairs. She would personally change the tires along the way as well as make any minor repairs.

On a rainy June 9, 1909, Ramsey and her female passengers posed for photographers in New York City. They wore driving veils and dusters (coats to keep the grit and sand from soiling their clothes). Then Ramsey cranked the engine (that effort alone required some strength), climbed into the Maxwell, adjusted her goggles, and started off on her adventure. She soon gained a top speed of 40 miles (64 km) per hour.

The Maxwell-Briscoe Company sent a reporter along in a pilot car that followed the

With a friend and two sisters-in-law as companions, Alice Ramsey traveled by car across the United States in 1909. Plagued by bad roads or no roads at all, flooding streams, flat tires, and mechanical failures, about the only obstacle she did not face was traffic. There were fewer than 130,000 cars in the entire United States at the time.

women. He filed reports from various stops along the way. Newspapers carried his frequent updates on Ramsey's progress. The reporter did not detail, however, the significant difficulties the Maxwell presented. Alice Ramsey did much more than change tires—though she would change about a dozen during the journey. She also cleaned spark plugs, tightened bolts, and scraped carbon from the combustion chamber. Rain in Iowa turned roads to deep mud. Then she and her friends, sometimes with help from the reporter in the pilot car, pushed the Maxwell out of the mud. At one point, when too deeply mired, they required the assistance of a local farmer whose team of horses dragged the car out of the thick mud. Ramsey once even crossed a river on the wooden ties of a railroad trestle, jarring her bones as well as the Maxwell's axles.

On August 7, 1908, Ramsey rolled into San Francisco, completing the journey in fifty-nine days. As the first woman to drive an automobile coast-to-coast, she triumphantly declared, "Women can handle an automobile just as well as a man."

They sit on stools at the marble-topped counter. There they discuss "the expedition." It was Betty's idea to form a summer Camping and Tramping Club. Betty was always dreaming up adventures for her chums (as young people in the early twentieth century often called their close friends). For two weeks, Betty explains, the girls will tramp 20 miles (32 km) a day! They will spend each night in a different camp. The cabins will be much more fun than a hotel, Betty tells them.

A few high school boys have been listening to the conversation. Percy speaks up. Twenty miles a day will be exhausting, he says, at least for a girl. "You never can do it," Percy says, "never!"

"Oh, yes, we can," says Betty, assuredly.

Much of real-life society in 1913, the year of the book's publication, would have agreed with Percy's opinion that girls didn't have the same physical stamina as boys. Betty's insistence that they do, however, challenges that social assumption. It also reflects the changing times. In other books in the series, the girls participate in outdoor activities that society had previously restricted to boys.

Each of the four "outdoor girls" in the series is a different type of person. Betty Nelson is outgoing and fun loving. Her chums have nicknamed her Little Captain because she is the one who takes charge of things. Grace Ford is indeed graceful. She is tall and

sophisticated, just like the Gibson girl on the magazine covers. She *loves* chocolates and eats so many that she sometimes gets indigestion. Amy is a talented musician who plays the piano. But she is timid and shy and murmurs when she speaks. Her chums think her sweet. Mollie, on the other hand, has a sudden temper. She is a risk taker, and she hates being bored. She drives her automobile at the reckless speed of 30 miles (48 km) an hour! She is a bit tomboyish, and her chums call her Billie.

As the leader, Betty is the character in each book who makes something happen. She gets the plot moving. Mollie's recklessness, on the other hand, often complicates the situation, creating suspense. The publisher of the Outdoor Girls series intended each character to appeal to a certain type of female adolescent reader. A timid or an artistic girl might relate to Amy. A girl who longs to be a willowy Gibson girl might relate to Grace. In real life, however, women are not so easily divided into four such simple categories as leader, risk taker, artist, or beauty.

The creator of the series was Edward Stratemeyer, who had a syndicate (agency) that provided series outlines to various authors. They then in turn wrote under pseudonyms. His books for boys were also very popular and included the Hardy Boys and the Tom Swift series. He realized that young girls too enjoyed leisure reading. So he created the

Bobbsey Twins series for them. As years passed, Stratemeyer realized that young women's lives were changing. Besides playing sports, such as basketball, they were also driving automobiles. In addition to the Outdoor Girls, Stratemeyer began creating other series, including the Motor Girls and the Moving Picture Girls. The characters in these series too were types, similar to Betty, Grace, Amy, and Mollie. Whether they were tramping or ice-skating outdoors, driving motorcars across the country, or solving mysteries on a movie set, these fictional heroines were all modern girls.

The grizzly bear became a dance rage once it was introduced in the Ziegfeld Follies (a Broadway song-and-dance show) in 1910. Not only did it require somewhat undignified bearlike movements, but the dancers were periodically required to yell out, "It's a Bear!"

The Animal Dance Craze

Dancing, too, was turning with the century. Ragtime music, with its syncopated, or somewhat irregular, beat and a bouncing melody became popular. As dance movements changed to fit the new rhythms, women's fashions changed. Greater locomotion required shorter skirts and less tightly laced corsets—or no corsets at all.

Among the most popular of the new dances was the South American tango. This dance was much different from a waltz, where a man and woman held each other far apart and only very lightly—her hand in his, his fingers lightly against her back. When dancing the tango, however, the man held the woman in the crook of his right arm. She held her head back, with her hand on his hip. During the winter of 1910, the tango became the new dance craze in New York City and soon spread across the country.

Supporters argued that dancing was excellent physical activity. It stimulated the heart and lungs, stated the director of Yale

Le Tango

NOT PERMITTED TO USE BEACH CH...

Medical advice aside, everybody loved the tango (left).
The elegant dance was performed everywhere from polite
Society's ballrooms to the beach at Coney Island in
New York City (above).

University's gymnasium program. Irene Castle, a ballroom dance instructor, believed that dancing could erase years of age from a woman. Opponents of dancing argued that the activity was a waste of time and could even harm a person's health. In 1914 a German doctor noted the "peculiar symptoms" of men and women who danced the tango. A dull ache in the front and lower part of the calf was the first symptom. Within a few days, the pain increased. Eventually, climbing and descending stairs became difficult. The doctor concluded that the unusual dance step of the tango, requiring a person to stretch the foot and toe muscles, inflamed the muscles. He called this new disease tango foot. He offered no remedy.

Dancing caused more serious ailments than just sore feet and legs, especially for women, at least according to a Dr. R. A. Adams. He wrote a book titled *The Social Dance* and described the physical effects of dancing on women:

Visit the dancing woman the day "after the ball is over;" hear her weak voice, and look into her listless eyes; note her general lassitude [weariness], observe that she has scarcely any life left in her, and you will get some idea of the physical effect of the dance. . . . If you will run over the list of the habitual dancing women of your neighborhood, no doubt you will find that they have more sick days, more female troubles, more nervous troubles, and more of general weakness than any other class of people.

The antidance crusaders believed that a woman's body was unable to endure the rigors of dance. They also believed that her moral character was in jeopardy on the dance floor. Dancing encouraged immorality, argued community leaders, as well as leaders of many religious faiths. While visiting New York City, the mayor of Boston, Massachusetts, was shocked by the type of dances he saw young men and women performing. They were hopping, dipping, sliding, and shivering. In some instances, the man and the woman danced cheek to cheek! The mayor returned to Boston and asked the women of his city to help "make war on the tango, the turkey trot, bunny hug, and the grizzly bear, and other animal dances." The dance craze debate extended to magazines. Even books were published for and against dancing.

the antidance crusaders believed that a woman's body was unable to endure the rigors of dance. They also believed that her moral character was in jeopardy on the dance floor.

The closeness and touching was one point of debate. Another was the dance halls where this physical activity took place. A respectable Society dance held in a fashionable ballroom was a far cry from the growing number of dimly lit and smoky dance halls where working girls gathered at night. A welfare committee for working girls visited a number of dance halls in New York City, many of which were open during the afternoons. According to an article in the *New York Times*, the women who served on this committee "shuddered" at what they had seen. A few weeks later, the committee presented its findings at a meeting attended by city officials, religious leaders, and social workers, among others. A Dr. Grant testified that dancing was a "complicated athletic activity." But he added, "Of all the dance halls in the city, there were not three that were fit for a girl to enter."

The committee insisted it did not wish to outlaw dancing. However, cleaner and more brightly lit dance halls were necessary. Needed, too, were social chaperones inside these dance halls to protect the working girls (none of whom apparently were on the committee or attended the meeting). Despite the efforts and good intentions of the antidance crusaders, dance halls flourished. The animal dances might have been vulgar, but they were fun.

By the second decade of the twentieth century, newspapers were printing articles on the influence of dance on fashions in Paris, France. When Parisian women began to dress for dancing, the rest of the world soon copied the

In this 1912 drawing by Herbert Johnson titled Turkey Trot, even the animals seem scandalized by the dancers' odd movements.

Parisian styles. The long, tightly laced corset was replaced by a rubberized girdle, which would stretch. Gone were the too-tight shoes that had resulted in tango foot. In their place were tango slippers, tied with ribbons. Gone too were rigid collars, heavy and stiff fabrics, and long trains. Instead, women began wearing collarless frocks made of softly swirling chiffon, with silk lingerie underneath.

By 1915 dance had reformed fashion. These new fashions, in turn, changed the way women took care of their clothing. Chiffon

SILKS—SATINS—LACE

Kept dainty and new through the longest vacationing

MADAME has given instructions to pack only the finest, the filmiest. The silk and valenciennes underthings and the sheerest of the stockings. The georgette frocks with their extravagantly simple air. Two favorite negligées and the loveliest of the blouses.

Always Madame refuses to be bothered with the great number of her possessions—only the most adored. For with Lux these few can be kept so fresh, so exquisite.

At the first speck of dinginess in filet collar or cuff, Marie tosses the beloved one into a big bowlful of Lux suds. The foamy bubbles cover it. The rich lather presses through and through it. Every tiny thread is searched out and cleansed snowy white.

In half an hour the pretty thing will be bright and sweet and summery again, looking as calmly new as if it had just come out of the specialty shop's tissue wrappings!

The old way of washing was so heartless. Many a fragile blouse has Madame wept over in the old days—actually scrubbed to death! But the Lux way is so different. It is so gentle, so careful with her fine things.

There's never a bit of pasty cake soap to stick to the silk thread and be ironed into it! Never a thought of a cruel rub! The pure suds just whisk the dirt away and leave the fabric whole and new, the color clear. The grocer, druggist or department store has Lux always ready for Madame. Lever Bros. Co., Cambridge, Mass.

How to launder silks

Whisk a tablespoonful of Lux into a thick lather in half a bowlful of very hot water. Add cold water till lukewarm. Dip the garment up and down in the rich lather. Squeeze the suds through it—do not rub. Rinse in three lukewarm waters. Roll in a towel. When nearly dry press with a warm iron. Jersey silk and georgette crêpe should be gently pulled into shape as they dry, and should also be shaped as you iron.

If you are not sure a color is fast, first wash a sample and dry it. If the color runs try to set it, as follows: For brown and black and pink use two cups of salt to a gallon of cold water. For blue use half a cup of vinegar. For lavender, use one tablespoonful of sugar of lead. Soak for half an hour and then rinse thoroughly before washing. Colors must be set before each washing.

LUX
LUX
for all fine laundering

A magazine advertisement for Lux laundering soap reflects the change in fabric that took place during the 1910s. Several suitcases would have been required for the heavy fabrics and stiffly tailored designs of the beginning of the decade. The ad shows a woman packing delicate, easily packed fabrics—much better suited for her new, more active lifestyle at the end of the decade.

and silk were delicate fabrics. A Lux soap advertisement in the *Chicago Tribune* in 1918 asked young women, "Are you still keeping on with the old-fashioned rub, rub, rub? Your grandmothers rubbed soap in and then rubbed it out on hard wash-boards." Fabrics of grandmother's day, such as muslin, were stiff and sturdy. But a modern girl wears "dainty things." To keep her fashions looking their best, she must wash them in Lux soap flakes.

Basketball and Bloomers

At the end of the nineteenth century, educators began to promote physical activity as necessary for a young woman's good health. Schools began building gymnasiums. Women exercised on parallel bars. The general philosophy of physical education was different for women than for men. Men played to win. Women exercised for their health.

In 1892 Dr. James Naismith, a physical education instructor at Springfield College in Massachusetts, invented a new indoor sport, basketball. According to the original thirteen rules of the game, no doubt, Naismith intended it as a man's sport. When Senda Berenson, a physical education instructor at Smith College, also in Massachusetts, read about the new sport, she organized a women's basketball program. She believed, as much of society did at that time, that women didn't have the physical stamina of men. She thought women should engage in moderate rather than strenuous exercise. Running was considered unladylike. So, too, was sweating. So Berenson altered the rules of play. She added an additional player (men's basketball rules indicated five players). She also divided the court into three fields, or zones. Two players covered each zone and could not move beyond the field's boundary.

The Great Underarm Campaign

At the turn of the century, women did not shave their legs or their underarms. The Gillette Company had been selling shaving products to men for many years, but the company began to look at women's new fashions and new physical activities and saw dollar signs. In 1915 Gillette came up with a new product called the Milady Decolletee razor. Giving a razor a more feminine form and name was easy. Convincing women that underarm hair was unsightly and unfeminine was the hard part. Society, in general, and the upper crust of society, in particular, didn't speak of women's underarms. It was vulgar to do so. Gillette's advertisements did not mention that part of a woman's body. They suggested its location through carefully chosen words, such as this statement from an advertisement in *Harper's Bazaar* magazine from May 1915: "Summer dress and Modern dancing combine to make necessary the removal of objectionable hair."

Gillette's great underarm campaign included other carefully selected words intended to persuade women without offending them. Instead of writing *shaved*,

Odo-Ro-No was a rare company that decided to take the direct approach to a delicate topic. Not only did it use the word Odor *in its product name, but the company referred to the product as "toilet water [perfume] for excessive perspiration." And in 1919, the company was the first to use the term "B.O." in an ad.*

advertisers used the word *smoothed*. Instead of writing *hair*, advertisers used the word *down*. (Down is soft, fine feathers on birds.) Historian Teresa Riordan says perhaps Gillette was responding to women's demand for a product created just for them. Or maybe Gillette created a new fashion trend of smooth underarms. Either way, by 1917 the company had sold more than one million Milady razors. "Smoothing" became part of a woman's daily beauty routine.

A girls' basketball team competes at the turn of the last century. Note that three forwards and three guards are clustered under the basket at one end of the court. (The woman in the white shirt is no doubt a coach.) Three more forwards and three more guards are waiting patiently at the opposite end of the court for the ball to come their direction. That way, none of the twelve young women will be required to strain herself by running more than half the length of the court.

The three zones meant that no woman player would be required to run the distance from one end of the court to the other. This reduced the amount of physical exertion and so kept the women from becoming exhausted. Berenson also prohibited the players from stealing the ball from one another. A player could dribble the ball but was only allowed three bounces.

The game proved to be very popular. By 1905 most women's colleges had taken it up with great success. Women in cities across the country had formed hundreds of basketball teams.

In a guidebook for women's basketball, published in 1905, Berenson emphasized the significance of basketball for women.

Women were proving their worth in the professions, she wrote, and "now that all fields of labor and all professions are opening their doors to her, she needs more than ever the physical strength to meet these . . . demands. And not only does she need a strong physique, but physical and moral courage as well." A woman's gym uniform was quite similar to what she would wear while sunbathing on a beach. Her loose, long-sleeved flannel blouse had a middy (or sailor) collar with a tie down the front. She wore pleated bloomers, baggy pants that came to just below the knee. She also wore dark cotton stockings and laced boots or lightweight slippers. Spectators of the game were other *before the game had been in progress five minutes, the referee called time-out while "the girls rearranged their hair and made needed repairs to their gymnasium costumes."*

—*New York Times*, February 11, 1905

women, since a woman wearing bloomers was something not to be viewed by men. Despite the rules that required ladylike play, the games often got rough. While the bloomer uniform allowed for freer movement, the slippers didn't provide much traction on a basketball court. The janitor might sprinkle ashes on the floor to give the women more grip and prevent bruises from falls and skids. Once a game got under way, the players often knocked into one another, resulting in more bruises, blackened eyes, and scraped hands. Hair came undone as hairpins dropped to the floor.

In reporting on a game between two young women's academies in New York City, a *New York Times* article noted that the athletes were "emulating [copying] their brothers" on the court. "Roughness was prevalent from the first toss of the ball," the article stated. Before the game had been in progress five minutes, the referee called time-out while "the girls rearranged their hair and made needed repairs to their gymnasium costumes."

Some students began wearing their bloomers to class. Of course, they wore a skirt over the bloomers, but still, the practice was a bit shocking.

Department Store Fantasies

Magazines were not the only means of showcasing women's fashions. Department stores were a magazine come to life. When a woman walked through the doors of Wanamaker's in Philadelphia, Macy's in New York City, or Marshall Fields in Chicago, she entered a world of fashion fantasy. The stores were large. Marshall Fields on State Street offered twelve floors of merchandise, more than 35 acres (14 hectares) of selling space. The shopping aisles were as wide as a boulevard. Glass windows and high ceilings, floor-to-ceiling pillars, chandeliers, and marble floors created "eye-dazzling extravagance." Elevators lifted the shoppers from the toiletries and linens displayed on the first floor to hats, lingerie, clothing, sports equipment, toys, furniture, and even food on the upper floors.

Best of all—admission was free. A

woman could look for hours and often did. Women primarily populated the stores. "A constantly arriving and departing throng of shoppers," women filled the aisles on every floor. An article published in 1910 advised merchants how best to display their items for sale. The author described the feminine hustle and bustle inside a department store: Buying and selling, serving and being served—women. . . . Behind most of the counters, on all the floors . . . women. At every cashier's desk, at the wrappers' desks, running back and forth with parcels and change, short-skirted women.

Within department stores, women of all social classes might mingle, though in truth, a working woman had little free time to spend looking. She might, however, stand before a department store window and gaze at the displays. At the time, these shop clerks, like all working women, were generally referred to as girls.

For the shopgirls who stood for as many as six hours at a time behind a counter—they were not allowed to sit, even if no customers were at their glass displays—life inside the emporium could be physically exhausting. Most clerks were single women who lived in the city. If they were careful, their earnings might be just enough to pay the rent on a boardinghouse room and buy meals—but usually not enough to purchase the glamorous items on display all around them.

The centerpiece of the Wanamaker's Philadelphia store was the Grand Court, site of the world's largest organ. The court seated fourteen thousand people. Seven floors of galleries overlooked the court, thereby making it possible for as many as twenty-five thousand people to listen to the organ.

The shopgirls wore a uniform. The shirtwaist and cinched skirt was uncomfortably tight, and underneath was a stiff corset. No soft slippers for these working women but rather heeled shoes that pinched the toes.

Airborne and Hobbled

On October 1, 1908, Edith Berg tied a rope around the bottom of her long, full skirt. Then she climbed onto Wilbur Wright's flying machine. Or maybe, she climbed onto the plane first and then tied the rope around her skirt. Either way, Edith Berg inspired a fashion trend: the hobble skirt.

At least, that is how the story goes. Berg was the first passenger to fly with Wilbur Wright on his experimental flying machine and, in doing so, became the first American woman ever to fly. She was airborne a full two minutes and seven seconds. She had tied the rope around her legs to keep her skirt from flapping over her head—and into the face of her pilot—while in flight. Berg did not at once untie the rope as she hobbled away from the flying machine, and a Paris fashion designer happened to spot her. He decided the modern age of transportation—airplanes and automobiles—required a new type of women's clothing, and he created the hobble skirt in Paris.

Paul Poiret's hobble skirt crossed the Atlantic Ocean, and women in the United States were soon hobbling down the street—and tripping and falling too. The skirt narrowed above the ankles, forcing women to take smaller strides. Some women tied a bit of rope around their calves underneath their skirt to ensure they would not take too large a step and risk tearing open a seam or, worse yet, injuring themselves.

Mrs. Hart O. Berg (Edith) made aviation and fashion history on October 1, 1908, when she took an airplane ride with Wilbur Wright, shown here at the controls of his flying machine.

Floorwalkers, or supervisors, moved among the shoppers. Their eyes were not on the merchandise, however. They watched the clerks and scolded one who did not smile, one who rubbed her aching neck or back, or one who slouched or leaned against the gleaming glass cases. Was her shirtwaist dirty? Were her shoes run-down at the heels? If so, the floorwalker might report her to management.

Image was everything inside the grand department stores. The clerks, too, had to present a fastidious image to the shoppers or risk losing their jobs.

The owner of Reiss Department Store of Mobile, Alabama, had his shopgirls photographed in October of 1914. He wanted to show that the age limit of his workers was very high. He did not believe in hiring children, as was common at the time.

No More Tootsey Wootseys

Some women rode bicycles or bounced basketballs. Some danced the grizzly bear or the turkey trot. Some tramped through the woods, and some fought against the consumption of alcohol. Still others marched in the streets, demanding the right to vote. Suffrage parades and demonstrations were another "outdoor" activity that engaged women at the turn of the century.

"Come on, Darling. Shoulder to shoulder. That's it. You do it like a soldier." So spoke a suffrage leader, encouraging her marchers to stay in line and keep pace. As many as five thousand women marched down New York City's Fifth Avenue on the afternoon of May 6, 1912. Most dressed in white and wore straw hats. Some carried banners. One read, "New York Denies the Vote to Criminals, Idiots, and Women."

On May 6, 1912, twenty thousand suffrage supporters joined a New York City parade, with half a million onlookers.

Along the sidewalks, people opposing suffrage jeered. The newspapers called them "antis" (as in antisuffragists). "Why don't you smile?" they shouted. "Go home and wash the dishes!" "Why aren't you minding the baby?"

Among the marchers were writers, college students, working women, and Society women. A few hundred men marched as well. A reporter from the *New York Times* reported that it was likely that the men marchers required more courage than the women in the parade. The mayor of New York City, however, was not among those courageous men. Nor did he sit in the reviewing stand. Mayor William Jay Gaynor and his wife had been "called out of town."

Newspapers covered the suffrage parade in New York City as well as other suffrage demonstrations elsewhere across the country that year and in the years that followed. In the 1910s, the debate both for and against women's suffrage was the stuff not only of newspaper and magazine articles but also of posters, pamphlets, editorial cartoons, and even humorous song lyrics.

What image of suffragists did the media promote? The images varied, depending on who created the message—the suffragists or the antisuffragists. For example, an antisuffrage poster stated in bold letters: "DANGER! Women's suffrage would double the irresponsible vote. It is a menace to the Home, Men's Employment and to All business."

The Teetotal Ladies

"Mrs. Nation Horsewhipped" read the headline in the *New York Times* on January 25, 1901. The short news story reported a fight the previous day between two women, Mrs. Carry Nation and Mrs. John Shilling (first name not reported), in Enterprise, Kansas. Shilling reportedly attacked Nation with a horse whip in the street, bruising her badly. Although both men and women witnessed the fight, none stepped forward to stop it. Police arrested both women. They charged Nation with disturbing the peace. Earlier, she had threatened to destroy a saloon with an axe, smashing its windows and hacking the whiskey barrels. The police arrested Shilling, the wife of the saloon manager, and charged her with assault. Since Nation had not, in fact, destroyed the saloon property, the court dropped the charges.

Armed with a Bible, a hatchet, and her forceful will, Carry Nation began her fanatical attacks on saloons after her first husband died of alcoholism.

Temperance societies, such as the Anti-Saloon League, had formed in the early nineteenth century to stop the sale and consumption of alcohol. Most of these organizations were religious. Members prayed, often in front of saloons, for the salvation of the poor "sinners" inside. Some members, such as Nation, became violent. Temperance organizations believed that the sale and consumption of alcoholic beverages was a source of many social problems. A husband who drank often spent all his money on booze rather than on his family. A drunken husband more often became abusive, beating his wife and children. Alcohol caused husbands and wives to divorce.

Both men and women supported the temperance movement. Yet the media portrayal of female temperance workers was often negative. Newspapers labeled these women as "cranks and fanatics." Kinder commentators referred to the women of the temperance movement as the "teetotal ladies." A teetotaler drank tea rather than alcohol. But the word's connotations suggested something else, as well. A teetotaler was an unlikable busybody—or worse, a tyrant—who tried to impose her strict moral views on others.

On the other hand, a pamphlet written by suffragist Jane P. Rogers in 1912 presented this fact: of the seventeen thousand teachers in the state of Wisconsin, 88 percent were women. Rogers asked, "If Wisconsin teachers are able to educate voters, why are they not able themselves to cast ballots? If Wisconsin teachers are able to educate the boys who are to become voters, why are they not able to educate girls who may do likewise?"

"Women are angels, they are jewels, they are queens and princesses of our hearts," stated Representative Charles D. Carter of Oklahoma in

"If Wisconsin teachers are able to educate voters, why are they not able themselves to cast ballots?"

—Jane P. Rogers, 1912

an antisuffrage speech in Congress. "Did angels and jewels and princesses spend their days in the kitchen?" the suffragists fired back. Women were flesh-and-blood human beings with minds and muscles too.

The New York State Association Opposed to Woman Suffrage believed women belonged in the home. It circulated a pamphlet to its members with this advice: "Tell every man you meet, your tailor, your postman, your grocer, as well as your dinner partner, that you are opposed to woman suffrage."

The suffragists argued that many women worked outside the home out of necessity. The "90,000 sewing machine operatives, the 40,000 saleswomen, the 32,000 laundry operatives, the 20,000 knitting and silk mill girls, the 17,000 women janitors and cleaners, the 12,000 cigar makers, to say nothing of the 700,000 other women and girls in industry in New York State" worked to put food on the table and pay the rent.

An antisuffrage poster asked, "Which do you prefer? The home or street corner for woman?" The poster showed two con-

Which do you prefer? This 1915 antisuffrage lithograph (above) shows a lovely mother and an unkempt suffragist. The suffragist media campaign was mainly focused on the issue of personal and political equality for women. The undated magazine drawing at right undermines the idea that women belong in the home.

trasting images of women. On the left was a mother with a neat hairdo kissing the baby in her arms. On the right was a woman whose hair has come undone. Her mouth was twisted into a grimace. She held a banner that announced a political rally. Portraying suffragists as ugly women was common. In some images, they were withered and thin and had Adam's apples protruding in their throat (a large Adam's apple is a masculine trait). In others, they were old and angry.

Suffragists complained not only of the ugly portrayals of feminists but also of the silly idealization of women in fashion magazines. "Women are no longer to be considered little tootsey wootseys who have nothing to do but look pretty," stated suffragist Lydia Commander. "They are determined to take an active part in the community and look pretty too."

And so the debate went—each side firing sharp words at the other. The editor of the most widely read women's magazine in the early twentieth century, *Ladies' Home Journal*, opposed suffrage. Edward Bok believed women lacked "the mental attitude" to understand business and political issues. They were emotional, impressionable, and impulsive. Bok controlled the content of what appeared in his magazines, sometimes inviting famous people to write articles that agreed with his views on subjects he felt were of concern to women and the nation. As a result, the articles in *Ladies' Home Journal* promoted the characteristics of "true womanhood": purity, piety (devotion), submissiveness, and domesticity.

Suffragist or Suffragette?

Suffragists had been fighting for the vote by peaceful means of negotiation and debate throughout most of the nineteenth century. A new figure in the suffrage movement, however, emerged in the first decade of the twentieth century. She was the suffragette. She was a rebel. Some thought her dangerous, and at times, she was.

The word *suffragette* first appeared in newsprint in the *Daily Mail* of London in 1906. The editor had written *ette* instead of *ist* intentionally, referring to a group of British women who were actively demonstrating for the right to vote in that country. The difference in the suffixes was significant. *Ette* means "small" or "diminutive." It can also mean "an imitation of something real." Calling a woman a suffragette was an insult, suggesting she wasn't a real suffragist at all. The suffragettes referred to in the *Daily Mail* of London were militant, willing to break the law and resort to violence to grab media attention. They threatened political leaders, interrupting their speeches and creating chaos during meetings. When police arrested them, they refused to pay their fines and instead chose to go to jail. While imprisoned, many staged hunger strikes to draw further attention to the lack of women's equality.

Taking a cue from their British sisters, American suffragists began adding more drama to their demonstrations. Here four young women carry a ballot box on a stretcher during a demonstration in New York.

Rather than being insulted by being called suffragettes, militant British women adopted the term as a badge of honor. The term's negative connotation stuck in the United States, however. The suffragists scorned the activities of the suffragettes because they felt that the sensationalized public demonstrations were doing more harm to the movement than good.

The British suffragettes, on the other hand, encouraged their American sisters to get militant. In time, many American women would also stage public demonstrations and endure imprisonment and hunger strikes. Their actions were never quite as violent, however, as those of the suffragettes in Great Britain.

In an article Sarah Bernhardt wrote for *Ladies' Home Journal*, the famous theater actress shared her views on suffrage and woman's rights. She believed women should have the right to vote because they

> *"Women are no longer to be considered little tootsey wootseys who have nothing to do but look pretty. . . . They are determined to take an active part in the community and look pretty too."*
>
> —suffragist Lydia Commander, 1905

were more patriotic than men. She thought women ought to become lawyers and physicians too. But this is where she drew the line.

She did not believe that women were physically equal to men. Because of their sex, she explained, women suffered ailments that men did not. She didn't use the word *menstruation*. No one in polite Society spoke of women's monthly cycles. Still, Bernhardt implied that menstruation was one of the "ailments." A woman's monthlies made her excitable and nervous. Many women reading *Ladies' Home Journal* would have agreed with the Broadway actress. They disapproved of women who bicycled, bounced basketballs, danced the grizzly bear or turkey trot, tramped through the woods, and marched in public protests. Suffrage was a complicated issue. By the second decade of the twentieth century, when the magazine published Bernhardt's article, it was becoming increasingly difficult to place women into one of two categories: prosuffrage or antisuffrage. No doubt Bernhardt's "middle of the road" sentiment—women should have rights but only so many—was typical of many American women.

It wasn't just men the suffragists had to convert. It was also the women, the fastidious women.

Chapter Three

AMUSEMENTS *of the* STAGE AND SCREEN

A 1900 vaudeville poster, Buffalo, New York

I don't care, I don't care,
What they may think of me.
I'm happy go lucky, Men say I am plucky,
So jolly and care-free.

—Jean Lenox, "I Don't Care," sung by Eva Tanguay, 1922

The outer office of a New York booking agency

looked like the waiting room of a train station. Dozens of people of all ages sat on benches. Some had yapping dogs dancing around their feet. Others held suitcases that contained instruments, stage props, or costumes. One or two might have munched on a doughnut or thick slice of bread for breakfast. Some were confident and cheerful. They laughed or chatted pleasantly. Others sat quietly alone, staring at the opposite wall or the clock, fearful that the wait would prove a disappointing waste of time.

The people gathered here were not passengers, though they traveled for most of the year. They were vaudeville performers. They were comedians, singers, dancers, cornet players, acrobats, magicians, ventriloquists, animal trainers, and other entertainers. A railing across one end of the room separated the performers from the office workers. Behind that was a closed door, leading to the private office of the booking agent who managed a group of theaters. He scheduled auditions for some waiting performers. He booked contracts for others. As the morning wore on, some in the waiting room got a shake of the head. The booking agent had nothing for them that day.

Vaudeville was one of the United States' most popular amusements at the turn of the century. It was a stage show with ten or sometimes as many as twenty acts that played continuously from morning until almost midnight. When the last act ended, the first act started again. Vaudeville meant variety. The acts on a bill, or program,

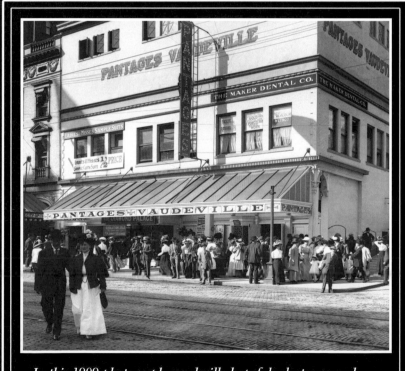

In this 1909 photograph, vaudeville hopefuls cluster around Pantages theater in Seattle, Washington, hoping for an opportunity to audition. This was the first theater to carry the Pantages name. Eventually there would be seventy such establishments either owned or controlled by Harry Pantages. Some of the theaters are still in operation almost a century later.

might include a dramatic reading, comic skits, song and dance routines, and a sprinkling of jugglers and jokesters. Benjamin Keith and Edward Albee ran the Keith-Albee theater circuit, one of the largest and most successful chains of vaudeville theaters on the East Coast. Vaudeville was wholesome family entertainment, they claimed. "I made it a rule at the beginning . . . that I must know what every performer on my stage would say or do," Keith stated. "If there was one coarse, vulgar, or suggestive line or piece of stage business in the act, I cut it out." In a 1914 article in the *New York Times*, Albee said, "The stages are run with the good manners of a ballroom."

Backstage at most vaudeville theaters was a sign that stated, "Performers must be in the theater one hour before their acts." Arriving on time wasn't the only rule of conduct inside a Keith-Albee theater. Another posted sign read, "If you have not the ability to entertain Mr. Keith's audiences without risk of offending them, do the best you can." Lack of talent was better than getting a laugh by insulting the audience, Keith lectured his performers. Performers, for example, could not use unacceptable terms such as "slob" or "son of a gun" onstage.

Keith and Albee were showmen. Their theaters were higher class and better managed than smaller vaudeville music halls. Still, Keith and Albee were in the business of making money, which meant persuading audiences to pay to see their performers. Convincing the public that vaudeville amusement was inoffensive to women and children meant more business and therefore more profits.

Albee also promoted the idea that vaudeville was "an ideal profession for women." The theater's audiences were respectable people from the community, he said. The backstage environment and dressing rooms were clean and safe. "Vaudeville is the one field in which

"Vaudeville is the one field in which women command a higher wage than men."
—*Edward Albee, 1914*

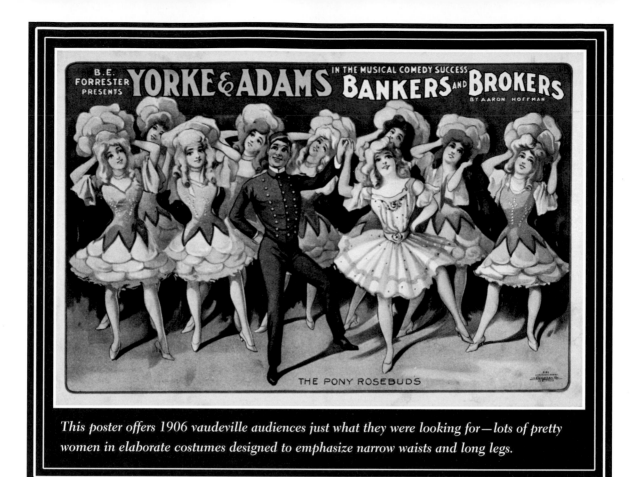

This poster offers 1906 vaudeville audiences just what they were looking for—lots of pretty women in elaborate costumes designed to emphasize narrow waists and long legs.

women command a higher wage than men," he correctly stated. Female performers' salaries were good, especially for the performers who got top billing, with their names printed in large, bold letters at the top of advertising posters. The headliner performed next to last on the program. A female headliner could earn as much as three thousand dollars a week or more. Even a newcomer, however, could earn one hundred dollars or more a week, Albee claimed. This was an amazing amount of money considering that women's work in other fields paid significantly less. In 1917, for example, a teacher might earn fifty dollars a month, or just under seven hundred dollars a year.

No wonder, then, that hundreds of women performers flocked to the booking agents' offices. They auditioned on bare stages in darkened auditoriums for the often bored managers who sat in the front row. The successful women got contracts and became road performers. The route from one theater to another in one city after another was called the circuit. They traveled most often by train, spending one or two nights in a city before moving on to the next engagement. Hitting the "big time" was earning a spot on the Keith-Albee circuit on the East Coast or the Orpheum circuit on the West Coast. Performers on all other circuits were regarded as "small time."

THE UPSIDE-DOWN LADY

"Her stage stunts would make most birds giddy," reported the *Indianapolis Star*. Ruth Budd's vaudeville act was a combination of gymnastics and music. She sang while flying through the air, often upside down. A Massachusetts newspaper described her performance as "rather sensational." At one point in her act, she hung by her toes from rings, and as she swung back and forth over the audience's heads, she sang.

By 1914, when Ruth Budd joined the Keith-Albee circuit, more and more American women were supporting the suffrage movement. Often billed on vaudeville programs as the Upside-Down Lady, Budd was also known as "the suffragist with steel biceps." That she believed women weren't the weaker sex wasn't so shocking. The Upside-Down Lady loved to prove wrong anyone who doubted her abilities. She claimed she could "pick up any man of twice my own weight and set him out on the sidewalk."

Ruth Budd is shown in 1916 wearing her white union suit, which was considered very revealing at the time.

She invited a newspaper reporter to touch her biceps, a shocking gesture. "Does this arm feel like a clinging vine?" she asked. He later reported that indeed her muscles were like steel. Whether she also lifted him over her head and deposited him outside on the sidewalk was not reported.

Budd delighted in shocking her audiences. She appeared first as a dainty woman in a dress. Then she put on a white leotard that revealed her muscular body before she began performing her impressive feats of physical strength.

Despite the newspaper claims of wholesome entertainment, many vaudeville acts were sexually suggestive. In reality, the manners of the stage were nothing like those of the ballroom. The audiences were not always from the best side of town. More often than not, they were from the working class. And the performers certainly were not always well behaved. Nor did the audiences particularly want them to be. French singer Yvette Guilbert appeared onstage in a Keith-Albee theater in Philadelphia in 1909 wearing a "billowing gown and long white gloves." She wore her hair swept up into a Gibson girl–style. Her appearance and behavior were indeed those of a fashionable woman. The audience, however, "sat on their hands," meaning they did not applaud. In New York, the people in the gallery (the cheapest seats) hissed and laughed at her "old-fashioned" clothing and refined behavior. In the slang of vaudeville, Guilbert was a flop.

In contrast, some of vaudeville's most popular stars of "the big time" were women whose acts were risqué. They wore revealing costumes and tights. So controversial were their acts that many outraged social reformers accused vaudeville of degrading American morals. Even so, vaudeville was the country's number one amusement at the turn of the century, and the entertainment could sometimes be downright scintillating.

The Bawdy Ladies

Eva Tanguay admitted she had little talent. She couldn't sing. She couldn't dance. What

Eva Tanguay, shown here in 1899 at the age of twenty, already shows the dramatic presence that will propel her to vaudeville fame in the next decade.

she had was an ability to shock and excite her audiences. In doing so, she generated a good deal of publicity for her stage acts. Her blond hair was frizzy, "a wild mop" described reporter Ada Patterson. Tanguay had a "large, smiling mouth and pertly turned up nose . . . small, impudent eyes. Every inch of her is alive." In 1904 Tanguay became known as the "I Don't Care Girl," after the song she sang of the same title became a big hit. She certainly didn't seem to care about her hair or the modesty of her clothing. Her stage costumes were sometimes made of feathers and veils, revealing her bare legs and arms. On occasion, she even wore costumes made of objects, such as pads of paper, pencils, or Lincoln pennies. She might not have been able to dance, but she could—and did—whirl, twirl, wiggle, and spin. The *New York Times* compared her movement onstage to a cyclone.

A bawdy woman was a naughty woman. She was naughty because of how she dressed onstage but also because of how she behaved onstage. Eva Tanguay was a bawdy woman. She sang songs with sexually suggestive titles and lyrics, such as "I Want Someone to Go Wild With Me" and "It's All Been Done Before, but Not the Way I Do It."

She also sang, "If I'm not successful, I won't be distressful, 'cos I don't care." But she was successful. "There was no doubt that she won her audience completely," reported the *New York Times* in 1913. At the height of her popularity, she earned as much as thirty-five hundred dollars for a performance.

"She came on like a meteor, but there is a lasting quality," wrote Ashton Stevens in the *Chicago Examiner* in 1911. What did she have that other female performers did not? Some said confidence and sheer nerve. Others wondered if she were insane.

Tanguay had a reputation for being just as brassy offstage. But her outrageous behavior was just part of the performance. She

What did Eva Tanguay have that other female performers did not? Some said confidence and sheer nerve. Others wondered if she were insane.

Mae West worked on the stage and vaudeville from the age of five. By the time she was fourteen, she must already have been very seductive, as she was billed as the Baby Vamp. Her later career was based on her wit combined with sex appeal, as highlighted in this caricature.

per headline the following day. Her madness, she said, was all about money. The more she was paid, the crazier her performances would be.

Although there wasn't anybody quite like Eva Tanguay, she wasn't the only bawdy woman of the stage. There was also, among others, Mae West.

Mae West appeared onstage in a dress that emphasized her hourglass figure (thanks to a tightly laced corset and equally tight gowns). A typical stage costume for West was a black velvet, hip-hugging gown trimmed with silver and rhinestones, which sparkled in the footlights. She often kicked aside the gown's long train with her shoe. She walked across stages in a sultry way, slowly, with one hand on her hip. She wore a large hat cocked to one side and decorated with ostrich feathers and other plumes. While performing, she raised her long fingers to her blonde hair and caressed it. Patting her hair was, in fact, part of her performance.

She was a wisecracker, delivering funny lines. "It isn't what you do," she told the audience, "it's how you do it." How she walked, how she touched her hair, and especially how she delivered her lines were provocative. When Mae West performed "If You Don't Like My Peaches, Don't You Shake My Tree" for vaudeville executive Edward Albee, she sang sweetly and batted her eyelashes innocently.

understood that temper tantrums could generate a press story and keep her name in print. Newspaper headlines reported on the vaudeville star's fines and arrests for a variety of abusive behaviors, including roughing up a theater worker and slashing theater curtains. In April 1908, she arrived in Baltimore, Maryland, for a two-week performance. Before going to the theater, she toured a few city streets to look at the advertising billboards. When she saw the names of other performers advertised but not her own, she turned right around and left the city. "Miss Tanguay Won't Play" was the newspa-

Black Vaudeville's Sweet Mama Stringbean

Ethel Waters was a teenager working as a maid and laundress in a Philadelphia hotel when friends encouraged her to enter a talent contest. In a soft, crooning voice, she sang the ballad "When You're a Long, Long Way from Home." That contest and that song would earn Waters a new career as a performer. Producers offered her ten dollars a week to join their circuit. They booked her as Sweet Mama Stringbean, because she was so tall and skinny.

Her first vaudeville performance was in the run-down Lincoln Theater in Baltimore in 1917 where audiences were often as bawdy as the stage acts. However, when Waters began to sing "Saint Louis Blues," sweetly and softly, the audience grew quiet. She was no wild woman shouting and shimmying on the stage. Her voice was melancholy, deep, and thick like honey. When she had finished, the audience did more than applaud. They tossed coins on the stage.

Waters was an African American. She and some other African American performers found work in white vaudeville circuits. However, in most southern states, laws prohibited the mixing of races in public venues. Black performers were barred from whites-only theaters. Black performers could not stay in the same hotels or eat in the same restaurants as white performers. And often the money they earned was less than what theater managers paid white performers. Waters's salary of ten dollars a week was far less than the one hundred dollars a week that Keith and Albee boasted their newcomers received.

Ethel Waters was one of many multitalented actresses who moved from vaudeville to recording artist to movie actress. In her movie career, she did her best to avoid the stereotyped roles that were available to African American actresses.

The Theatre Owners Booking Association (TOBA) operated a black vaudeville circuit. But again, the conditions as well as the pay were often poor. Performers put up with one-night-only contracts, cheap hotels, dilapidated theaters, and long "jumps" (many miles) between performances. Black performers called the circuit Tough On Black Actors. Black female performers such as Bessie Smith and Ma Rainey got their start in vaudeville. Their singing would influence generations of musicians throughout the twentieth century.

He saw nothing vulgar in the performance. Onstage, however, her body movements and her tone of voice gave the same words a sexual connotation. Somehow she wasn't talking about a peach tree—and her working-class audiences loved it. She sang. She did a "shimmy" dance, shaking the top and bottom of her hourglass body. But the popular appeal of Mae West's vaudeville act was her bawdy personality.

Florenz Siegfeld's claim to having invented the Broadway showgirl may be exaggerated. But he did refine the concept. He paired carefully crafted shows with a strict code of behavior for the performers. Even though they were dressed outrageously and sometimes scantily, the Broadway showgirls seemed much more elegant than vaudeville's bawdy ladies.

Anna Held and the Ziegfeld Showgirls

Vaudeville stages were not the only public amusements where women at the turn of the century displayed their bodies. The showgirls of the Broadway theaters in New York City also exposed flesh. But these showgirls belonged to a different class of entertainment than did vaudeville's bawdy ladies.

In November 1915, the *Louisville Herald* quoted producer Florenz Ziegfeld as saying, "I invented the showgirl." But did he? There were plenty of chorus girls dancing and singing on stages across the United States before Ziegfeld began staging his extravagant shows. Ziegfeld's *showgirls*, however, didn't sing, dance, or even kick their legs. Instead, they appeared in lavish costumes and simply stood or moved gracefully across the stage. Their parade before the audience and their outrageous costumes emphasizing the female body were sensual but not bawdy. These showgirls were popular.

Newspapers wrote stories about them. Novelists wrote sentimental romances about the woes and temptations of life backstage.

The Ziegfeld showgirl, or chorine, would become a symbol of the modern American woman: independent but feminine, a performer but a lady as well. Dressed in elaborate costumes and performing simple choreographed movements (most planned or approved by Ziegfeld), the Ziegfeld girl would set new standards of beauty for American women—based on Ziegfeld's very specific vision. The ideal American woman was white. She was a true American, a woman born in the United States to parents who were also born in the United States. In other words, she was not an immigrant from Ireland, Italy, Poland, or Mexico. There were no women of color on Ziegfeld's stage. He searched for showgirls with "complexions like fresh cream and hair like twenty dollar gold pieces." He preferred them thin and slinky. His "ideal girl" had specific body measurement too: a 36-inch (91 cm) bust, a 26-inch (66 cm) waist, and 39-inch (99 cm) hips.

Anna Held took the pinched waist to the extreme. She actually had a rib removed surgically so that her steel and bone corset could pinch her waist to 18 inches (46 cm).

Ziegfeld imposed some strict offstage rules of conduct for his showgirls. They could not expose their skin to the sun and risk burning or tanning. They could not speak or act in a vulgar way. They had to wear gloves, hats, and high heels as women in polite Society did. Those who broke the rules risked losing their jobs. Ziegfeld had plenty of beautiful women waiting in line for the opportunity to join the show.

His first shining star was Anna Held. She also became his wife. Interviews with the Parisian beauty soon after her arrival in the United States in 1896 painted a portrait of a very feminine woman. Reporters wrote that her "chiefest charm is great, hazel eyes, over which hang long curtains [eyelashes], deeply fringed." She rode a bicycle but often fell off, reporters revealed. She thought knickerbockers (a type of loose-fitting pants gathered just below the knee) were shocking, and she'd never wear them again. To maintain her glowing skin, she bathed in milk—vast quantities of milk—every other day. What the reading public did not know, at least not for some time, was that Anna Held had been born in Poland and her father was French and Jewish. He had moved the family from Poland to France when Anna was a child. Ziegfeld knew that a Parisian chanteuse (singer) was more glamorous than a Polish immigrant, so he portrayed her that way. The new image also hid her Jewish heritage and avoided having to deal with turn-of-the-century prejudice in the United States against Jewish people.

Anna Held was a Gibson girl come to life (albeit a short one, as she was only a little more than 5 feet (1.5 m) tall.) Her corseted figure created the Gibson's "S" silhouette—bosom thrust forward, buttocks pushed back, and a waist as tiny as a wasp's. Held, too, was independent and could be haughty—and even a little bit naughty. The milk baths were publicity events planned by Ziegfeld, who arranged to have milk delivered at the same time he knew reporters would be there to interview his star. She often appeared onstage in some very un-Gibson-like outfits. In one act, her costume included a huge peacock tail spread like a fan behind her.

Anna Held was for a time Ziegfeld's most famous shining star, but she was not the only woman Ziegfeld celebrated on the American stage. With his wife's help, he created a sort of "high class" vaudeville show. "Your American girls are so beautiful, the most beautiful girls in the world," Held told her husband. She suggested he dress them in lavish costumes and parade them onstage. He took her advice and in 1907 created the first Ziegfeld Follies. Although the revue of acts featured singing and even some drama and comedy skits, the stars of the Follies were the showgirls. And not just a few—as many as fifty women appeared onstage at the same time. Often they descended long staircases wearing high heels and towering headdresses. They didn't walk. They glided with hips thrust forward.

Ziegfeld produced a new revue each year. Audiences waited in anticipation to see the showgirls and their imaginative costumes. Depending on the revue's theme, they might portray aviators or baseball players. In a number called "Taxicab Girls," the chorines' costumes represented motorcars (complete with headlights strategically placed over their breasts). In 1909 the showgirls' costumes represented each state of the union. Some wore miniature battleships for headdresses. In other revues, the chorines portrayed abstract ideas, such as happiness, gaiety, vanity, or kindness. The spectacular costumes were expensive, but audiences crowded the theater every year.

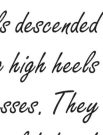

What did it mean to be selected by Florenz Ziegfeld to become one of the showgirls in one of his Follies? It meant more than just having work in an industry where thousands of beautiful young women hoped to make a living. It was an honor, a badge of beauty. The *New York Mail* put it this way: "Once Flo sizes up a girl, accepts her and puts her in a Follie . . . that girl bears forever a hallmark just as plainly as though a device were stamped upon her lovely arm."

Often the showgirls descended long staircases wearing high heels and towering headdresses. They didn't walk. They glided with hips thrust forward.

The Flickers Find Their Fans

Another type of American amusement was creeping into the cities in the first decade of the twentieth century. The nickelodeon (so called because admission cost a nickel) was a small shop or backroom theater where movies were shown. The owner of the nickelodeon cranked the projector machine by hand. Nickelodeons offered working-class Americans cheap entertainment. The moving pictures were silent, ran about ten to fifteen minutes, and changed every day. Within a few years, thousands of nickelodeons operated in cities across the United States. So popular were the nickel films that *Billboard* magazine called this fast-growing amusement the "jack-rabbits of public entertainment." The nickelodeons soon gave way to longer films and larger movie houses. Films began to be printed on celluloid, an early form of plastic, and because the images sometimes flickered, early motion pictures were sometimes called flicks, or flickers.

The popularity of moving pictures alarmed some social reformers and religious leaders. The flickering images were hypnotic, they charged. The dark movie houses bred inappropriate behavior between young men and young women. Some schoolteachers objected that children who spent their evenings at movie houses came to school exhausted. Nevertheless, going to the movies was a very popular pastime. According to film historian Steven J. Ross, "By 1914, every American town with a population over 5,000 had at least one movie theater." By 1920 approximately half of the U.S. population—as many as 50 million people—were going to the movies at least once a week.

Movies were so new and such an exciting technology that people often gasped in amazement at the images flickering on the screen. To illustrate this point, consider the news story of "The Housefly that Panicked Pittsburgh," published in the *New York Call*. A common housefly apparently landed on a movie projector's lens and was "magnified

Nickelodeon theater owners flashed frequent reminders onto their screens indicating that they would not tolerate the rowdiness of a vaudeville audience. Fashionable ladies had to be encouraged to remove their elaborate hats as well.

several hundred times" onto the screen. "Women and children screamed in terror, and a rush was made to the door by the panic-stricken audience," the newspaper reported. Within just a few years, Americans would develop more movie savvy. They understood that what was on the screen was fantasy, not reality. Even so, moving pictures engaged audiences in a way that other amusements could not.

Movies were silent. The film industry did not yet have the technology to incorporate sound or dialogue with the images. Title cards were lines of text projected on the screen, usually on a black background for easy reading. They provided information necessary for the audience to understand the basic story elements of character, setting, and plot. At times, the title cards included dialogue. During the silent film era, which lasted until 1927, acting was physical and emotional rather than verbal. The silence created a sense of "peeping through a keyhole," said film historian Jeanine Basinger. This "secret watching, silent sharing," as she called it, allowed audiences to feel as if they were there, a part of the action.

The movement of moving pictures also contributed to an audience's becoming involved in the story and characters on the screen. The camera could and did move in for close-up shots of actors' faces. Someone sitting in a theater balcony during a play could never get that close to the players on the stage or see such details of facial expressions. Moviegoers could view the same movie and the same images over and over and so begin to feel as if they knew the characters.

American amusement would never be the same. Movies changed how people perceived themselves, including how they perceived

The flickering images were hypnotic, critics charged. The dark movie houses bred inappropriate behavior between young men and young women.

A *still from the 1918 movie* Too Many Ladies *shows a full range of stereotypes: the good girl pulling her husband away from the temptress while the frilly maid looks on.*

women. There had been stardom before, said film historian Basinger. After all, performers such as Eva Tanguay, Ethel Waters, and even the Broadway theater actresses Sarah Bernhardt and Maud Adams were celebrities whose names and images appeared in newspapers across the country on a frequent basis. But moving-picture stars would, in time, shine brighter than the vaudevillians, the players on Broadway, and even Ziegfeld's fashion-show parade of beauties. One of the very first to shine brightly enough to earn the term moving picture star was Mary Pickford.

Virgins and the Vamps on the Silver Screen

Mary Pickford was called America's sweetheart. Before that, however, she was a "Biograph Girl." Biograph was a moving-picture production company. Biograph had a policy of not listing the "players" on its advertising posters and often not on its title cards either. Mary Pickford changed that. Moviegoers loved her innocent face. They loved her long, corkscrew curls. Soon Biograph realized that Pickford was attracting attention, and the company began to feature her in leading roles and to print her name as well.

Newspaper reporters gushed over Mary Pickford. A reporter described her behavior during an interview this way: She "wrinkled her pretty little forehead," she hung her head "with its little-girl curls," and she cast her eyes up "in that shy, appealing way of hers."

Movie fan magazines also promoted moving-picture stars. They often used flowery metaphors, Basinger noted. Mary Pickford, for example, was "every little girl's dream, white kid gloves and white tulle, a playground and children's laughter." The author's choice of words suggested that Pickford was feminine (white gloves and tulle) and innocent (children laughing in a playground). Pickford's characters were indeed childlike. In some films, such as *Rebecca of Sunnybrook Farm* and *Pollyanna*, she portrayed adolescent girls even though she was in her twenties.

Pickford received as many as 150 fan letters a day. Many mothers wrote to ask her advice on whether their daughters should become actresses. She did not tell reporters what she wrote to those mothers. But she admitted that at times she wished she were just an ordinary shopgirl working in a department store. Being a celebrated actress was exhausting.

Lillian Gish was also a star of early silent films. Both Gish and Pickford had begun acting as children, out of financial necessity. As teenagers, they moved from the stage to the screen. Lillian Gish, too, was the subject of flowery prose. One writer compared her to the "fragrant April moon of men's hopes" and her eyes to "butterflies fluttering softly to their object." Her roles were "the

In April 1909, Biograph director D. W. Griffith offered young Mary Pickford a salary of ten dollars a day—twice what most actresses were making. Her first film was shot in June and released in July. By the end of that year, Pickford had appeared in a total of forty-one films.

Lillian Gish (left) *made a career of being the fragile female—a heroine who overcomes all manner of suffering by being good and beautiful. Theda Bara* (above), *on the other hand, was the ultimate vamp (note the fingernails). Her specialty was bad-girl roles, which she carried off brilliantly, given the fact that she never spoke on-screen.*

essence of femininity." She played a pretty, innocent girl harassed by villainous men.

"Mostly in these movies I was a virgin," Gish said. "We tried for virginity in mind, in looks, in body, in movement." She often tired of the image, but her fans adored her in these roles of innocent and virtuous women. She found it difficult to hold an audience's interest using "goodness" only. "Goodness becomes dull quickly," she said. "It's so much easier to win an audience with a little wickedness."

Actress Theda Bara knew exactly what Lillian Gish meant. She—or rather her cel-

luloid characters—were the opposite of innocent womanhood. Theda Bara portrayed a type of movie character called a vamp. *Vamp* was short for *vampire*, and *vampire* means "a woman who is evil but attractive and lures good men to their destruction." A reporter noted that Theda Bara had the looks that went with such roles. "It would be squandering her resources to cast her in a Mary Pickford sort of role," stated a reporter.

Her "resources" were her dark, thick hair; her clothing; and her name. She was a midwesterner, born Theodosia Goodman in Ohio. That's not what the movie studios and fan magazines told their fans, however. Studio executives changed her name (a practice common for people in show business—Mary Pickford was born Gladys Smith, for example). They created a mysterious past for her. They said she was an Italian Arabian princess who had been born at an oasis at the foot of the Sphinx, an ancient Egyptian monument. Her name Bara was *Arab* spelled backward, and it supposedly meant "death." The movie studios called her Serpent of the Nile. For her roles, the filmmakers dressed her in veils, furs, and silks. They outlined her eyes with dark makeup.

Whereas Mary Pickford gazed shyly on the screen, Theda Bara sneered scornfully. Whereas Lillian Gish batted her eyelashes, Theda Bara petted a python. Pickford and Gish's characters were vulnerable victims. Bara's characters were vicious avengers. Like Pickford and Gish, Bara received letters from moviegoers—mostly angry correspondence from wives who thought Bara was a menace to men. Yet whenever these actresses tried to escape from the stereotypical roles given them, the fans objected. When Mary Pickford cut her "little-girl curls" in the 1920s, fans reacted as though she had committed a crime. When Bara played the courageous Juliet in Shakespeare's *Romeo and Juliet*, fans protested. Theda Bara was a vamp, and a vamp she'd always be.

Parlor Songs and Sheet Music Images

Whether performing on a vaudeville stage, in a Broadway theater, or on the movie screen, female performers inspired popular music. Composers and publishers wrote songs for these performers or tried to convince them to perform their songs. A vaudeville performance of a song could translate into thousands of sales of sheet music across the United States. The Ziegfeld Follies inspired parlor songs. Playing parlor songs on a piano at home and singing along was a popular American amusement.

This 1906 sheet music cover captures several popular themes of the decade: roses, Gibson girl hairdos, and the word dainty, which was an advertising buzzword implying all that was feminine.

The images on the sheet music as well as the lyrics were sentimental, such as "Mother was my best friend" and "The moon never beams without bringing me dreams of that wonderful mother of mine." The images of mothers printed on sheet music were of older women, white haired and gentle, sometimes in rocking chairs and sometimes knitting.

Young women, on the other hand, were often compared to roses. That could be a good thing, for roses were sweet, soft, and delicate. Or it could be not so good, for roses also had thorns. In "The Rose That Made Me Happy Is the Rose That Made Me Sad" (1913), a young man laments over the woman who loved him and then left him.

A few women could be vamps, as suggested by the song "On the Level You're a Little Devil, But I'll Soon Make an Angel of You" (1918). And yes, every word was part of the title. Theda Bara inspired the lyrics of "Rebecca Came from Mecca": "She's as bold as Theda Bara; Theda's bare but Becky's bare-er." More often than not, however, women were portrayed as innocent rather than malicious vamps in these parlor songs, especially the ballads. The emphasis on women being childlike is reflected in "Pretty Baby" (1916). The song begins, "Ev'rybody loves a baby, that's why I'm in love with you, Pretty Baby."

Amusements of the stage and screen did not erase the popularity of parlor music. Throughout the century, the music would change—not just the lyrics but the sounds and rhythm of music as well.

Chapter Four

IMMIGRANTS &
Other Working Girls

An unskilled, friendless, almost penniless girl of eighteen, utterly alone
in the world, I was a stranger in a strange city. . . . I was a waif and a
stray in the mighty city of New York. Here I had come to live and to toil.

—Dorothy Richardson, *The Long Day*, 1905

"MARRIAGEABLE GIRLS COMING!"

announced the *Newark Advocate* on September 20, 1907. The Newark, Ohio, newspaper reported that the young women were traveling aboard the steamship *Baltic*. The ship had departed from Liverpool, England, carrying 5,000 passengers. Exactly 1,002 of those passengers were single women and widows. The same article had appeared in the *New York Times* a day earlier. Other newspapers around the country also printed the story.

When he read about the female cargo aboard *Baltic*, a farmer in Kansas immediately wrote a letter to the vice president of the steamship company that owned the ship. He was a widower who wanted a new wife, he said.

He instructed the man to send one of the women "the minute the *Baltic* gets in" port.

Single women were among the many hundreds of thousands of people who immigrated to the United States in the nineteenth and early twentieth centuries. Many immigrants came because they were forced out by hard times in their native countries—famine, war, and religious intolerance. Others came because they were attracted by the American dream—owning land, finding work, and becoming wealthy. Another immigration attraction was American bachelors. In 1848 an immigration brochure encouraged single women and widows to come to

The Baltic *arrived in port on September 27, 1907, with a cargo of one thousand young women, a few of whom are shown above.* "GIRLS SEEK HUSBANDS" *shouted a* Washington Post *headline the following day. The article said that the young women were of "marriageable age and inclination . . . and on a grand husband hunt." Facing page: New York City telephone operators, 1901*

the United States to find a husband. One publication stated, "Industrious and calm girls who are at least reasonably good looking can be sure that they will receive several proposals of marriage in the first year." Women who had found husbands after coming to the United States wrote home with the encouraging news that "here are a good many men who want wives."

At the turn of the century, the letters from lonely single men continued. A German immigrant wrote to his aunt in the early twentieth century, describing the sort of wife he wanted. "My demands for a young woman are very limited, a developed figure with passable face is sufficient, everyone wants industriousness and a good disposition, social position and class make no difference."

The "marriageable girls" traveling on the *Baltic* hailed from many countries and not just Great Britain. When the ship arrived in New York City on September 27, bachelors had gathered to greet and meet them. A band played popular songs of the times.

News reporters and photographers also met the women. These "flowers" had dressed in their finest clothes for their arrival in the United States. They wore suits with long skirts and fitted jackets, hats brimming with flowers and large ribbons. All wore their hair pinned up. Some were young, and some were older. A few widows came with their children. Young and old, the marriageable women leaned over the ship's railings and smiled into the cameras. A reporter from the *New York World* asked Susan Thompson what kind of husband she hoped to find. "I like tall men and blondes," she answered. Then she laughed long and hard. Agnes McGirr described the man she hoped would marry her: a farmer with dark hair, at least thirty years old so that he'd "have some sense," and earning about one thousand dollars a year. Most of the immigrant women expected to travel farther inland

"It's a Pittsburgh millionaire for me."

—"Shipload of Girls Seek Husbands Here," *New York Times*, 1907, quoting an immigrant woman across the United States, settling in Michigan, Illinois, Iowa, and Kansas, among other states. Nellie O'Brien from Ireland fancied going to Pittsburgh, where, she'd heard, all the American men are millionaires.

If the single women had grand expectations for the American husbands they hoped to marry, the *World* also painted an idealistic picture of what these future wives could do. The reporter wrote: "They can cook, sing and play the piano, scrub, take care of a house and mind children, milk cows, raise chickens, weed garden beds, go to market, sew, patch and knit, make cheese and butter, pickle cucumbers and drive cattle."

Make no mistake, these immigrant women were working women. They had not come to the United States for love or romance. Marriage was a convenience, a way for them to find security and make ends meet. A woman traveling alone, even if accompanied by other women, was not without risks. The ocean voyage itself might result in illness or sometimes death. Upon arrival, a single or widowed woman had to find a place to sleep and eat. It is uncertain how many of the *Baltic*'s cargo of "marriageable girls" found a hus-

band and security. For those who did find a man and if that man proved to be a good companion, then likely the journey across the ocean had been worthwhile.

AMERICANIZING WOMEN

Many thousands of immigrant women came to the United States at the turn of the century. Many of those from Europe and the Middle East landed at Ellis Island in New York City's harbor. Not all images of immigrant women, however, were as flattering as

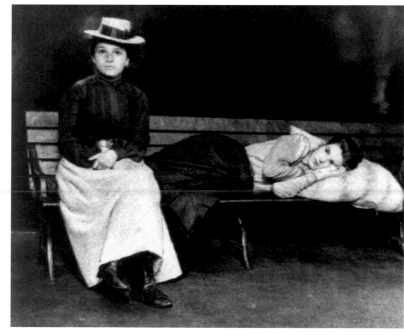

These women are being held at Ellis Island in 1902. They have been told that they are undesirable immigrants and they are to be taken back by the steamship company that brought them.

Immigrant women await processing at Ellis Island. If they pass a physical examination and if their legal papers are in order, they will be allowed to enter the United States.

were the photographs of and articles about the *Baltic*'s "marriageable girls." For others, no brass bands played for them upon their arrival. No photographers or reporters told their stories. The women and children who disembarked at Ellis Island wore the clothing of their native countries—Poland, Russia, Italy, Germany, Czechoslovakia, and Sweden. Many had been peasants, and their clothing was simple and practical. Rather than hats brimming with flowers, these women wore shawls or scarves tied over their heads.

The reaction to these immigrants varied. Some Americans wished to limit immigration or close the door completely to newcom-ers. Politician Thomas Watson described the mass of immigrants coming to the United States as "dangerous and corrupting hordes" who were planting seeds of "vice and crime" within city neighborhoods.

But even those Americans who supported the government's immigration policy were often prejudiced against foreign-ers. Many immigrants did not speak English, and some lacked formal schooling, so people thought them ignorant or stupid. Many immigrants were poor. They arrived with only a few belongings. They rented cheap rooms in crowded tenement buildings in neighborhoods where other immigrants had also settled. Because the tenements often lacked sanitation, people tended to believe that the immigrants too were unclean. Because newcomers clung to their native cultures, including eating foods from their homeland, some people thought them un-American and a threat to democracy.

Immigrants arrived on the American West Coast as well. Many had come from China and Japan. They, too, settled in ethnic neighborhoods. Newspaper headlines about San Francisco's Chinatown focused on vices such as gambling and drug use, specifically opium use. Immigrants from both coasts flowed into the nation's interior regions, creating even more suspicion. Chinatowns formed in many midwestern cities, including Chicago. A Chicago newspaper reported that sanitation inspectors had found within the Chinatown section of that city "dozens of opium dens . . . teeming with filth." They feared, the headline stated, that the dreaded disease called the plague would erupt in these filthy hovels and spread throughout the city.

A 1910 photograph by Lewis W. Hine captures the plight of an immigrant woman and her children. They sit on a bed in a windowless rear bedroom of their tenement apartment on the Lower East Side of New York City. The pots have been placed around the room to catch the water dripping through leaks in the ceiling.

Immigrants also crossed from Mexico into the southwestern states. Here, too, racist attitudes toward immigrants existed. A reporter for the *Saturday Evening Post* painted a grim picture of an immigrant neighborhood in Los Angeles, describing it as "endless streets crowded with the shacks of illiterate, diseased, pauperized Mexicans . . . on the ragged edge of starvation."

Social reformer Jacob Riis wrote about a classroom in a public school on New York City's Lower East Side. This neighborhood was home to hundreds of thousands of immigrants. Daily, the teacher asked the children, "What must you do to keep healthy?" Riis wrote that the whole school responded with a sing-song chant they had learned:

I must keep my skin clean,
Wear clean clothes,
Breathe pure air,
And live in the sunlight.

But who would fetch the water and boil it free of dirt so a child could bathe or wash clothes? Soap was not always affordable when there was rent to pay and hungry mouths to feed. Although the children had learned the answer, they knew little of baths. As for fresh air and sunlight, the tenement buildings stood shoulder to shoulder and rose so high as to shadow the streets.

There was another part of the immigrant story, Riis believed. Stories of heroic immigrants were often omitted from the daily newspapers, he stated. "And yet it is not an uncommon thing to find sweet and innocent girls, singularly untouched by the evil around them, true wives and faithful mothers." Thousands of immigrants, he wrote, were "laboring earnestly to make the most of their scant opportunities for good."

Like many immigrants, Chinese immigrants to the United States clustered together both by choice and necessity. They wanted to maintain their culture but also wanted the safety of banding together against the sometimes violent racial prejudice they encountered. These clusters eventually grew to large urban neighborhoods known as Chinatowns. The photo shows New York City's Chinatown in 1909.

In 1920 the Young Women's Christian Association (YWCA) studied the "immigration problem." In particular, the investigating committee wanted to determine the best way to help and protect the two hundred thousand immigrant women and children who came to the United States each year. The committee made recommendations on how to assimilate immigrant women—that is, Americanizing them by teaching them the language and culture of their new country. Learning English was a critical first step. Helping the women find employment was another.

San Francisco's Chinese YWCA also promoted Americanization through classes and club activities. In cities where large numbers of Mexican immigrants settled, social reformers established programs with the specific intent of changing the lifestyles of the immigrants. These programs targeted women and children but especially mothers. Mothers were the moral guardians of the home. Once an immigrant mother embraced the American way of life, reformers believed, she would pass the American values to her children. "'Go after the women' should become a slogan among Americanization workers," stated one teacher of immigrant Mexican girls, "for after all the greatest good is to be obtained by starting the home off right." In addition to teaching English-language skills, Americanization programs included courses on cooking, homemaking, hygiene, the U.S. government, and job skills.

> Mothers were the moral guardians of the home. Once an immigrant mother embraced the American way of life, reformers believed, she would pass the American values to her children.

Americanization programs had some success, but many failed. One reason for failure was the organizers' ethnocentric attitude that foreign cultures were of no value in the United States. For Mexican women, Americanization meant (among other things) replacing their traditional foods with American foods, such as bread instead of tortillas or lettuce instead of beans. This they resisted.

THE MOTHER INSTINCT

"The mother instinct is exceedingly strong in Mexican girls," wrote Pearl Ellis in a 1929 book titled *Americanization through Homemaking*. "They begin by mothering little brothers and sisters, of whom there are many."

The book was intended for social reformers working with Mexican women immigrants. The language reflects assumptions many social workers had about Mexican women. "Most Mexican women feel that if they have not borne a child they have not fulfilled their mission in life," the book stated. "Mexican girls are very fond of sewing." Statements like these may not seem harmful. Yet such sweeping generalizations led to the unfair assumption that young Mexican women might become mothers and even work in sewing factories, but they wouldn't achieve much more than that.

Ellis's book also suggested that Mexican girls were malnourished, but not because they didn't eat. They did not eat "the right variety of foods" to promote growth and healthy development. They ate Mexican fare and not American food. The handbook noted too that Mexican women were known for their clean laundry. Their children, however, were another matter. "Children are also noted for being dirty in appearance most of the time," the author stated. She declared that the amount of time and energy Mexican mothers spent washing tubs of clothing could be put to better use by teaching their children clean habits. Although condescending and at times downright mean spirited, *Americanization through Homemaking* reflected the attitude many Americans held toward Mexican women and their children in the early 1900s.

Social reformer Emily Greene Balch warned that assimilation of immigrants—whether male or female—was bound to fail if the United States forced people to forget their heritage. What was needed was more than classroom lessons and sing-song chants about fresh air and clean clothes. Emily Balch and women like her, including Jane Addams and Lillian Wald, formed settlement houses and opened missions in the same crowded and often unsanitary neighborhoods where immigrants lived. They offered social services to women and children and invited them into their homes and into their classrooms.

Jane Addams, shown here in 1913, was a college graduate from an upper-class family. She felt a strong sense of social responsibility. Among her many accomplishments was the founding of Hull House (a settlement house) in Chicago. She also successfully worked to pass the nation's first juvenile justice law.

RESCUES ᴁ RACISM IN CHINATOWN

On a snowy April morning in 1905, a plainly dressed woman "threaded" her way through the congested alleys of New York City's Chinatown. Men turned and scowled at her as she passed. Women leaned from their shambling tenement windows to stare down at her. The woman climbed the steps of a building marked Number 34 and "disappeared in a dark doorway." The Chinese hated this particular white woman. Some had threatened to murder her. Still, she was not afraid. She lived among the Chinese people because she wanted to help them. Her name was Helen F. Clark.

The *New York Times* had recently published a flattering profile of Clark. The reporters used language to create a glowing image of a selfless woman dedicated to helping others. She was a "rescuing angel" and "a good Samaritan." The reporter wrote, "Through dens of vice she makes her endless way, exhorting and imploring, always quietly, always gently, always beautifully." In the same article, however, Chinese women were portrayed as helpless victims of Chinese masters or opium addiction. Some women and children were slaves, bought and sold like property. Often using sensational language, the reporter described the fate of two such children, both of whom Helen Clark had rescued. Clark discovered seven-year-old Ah Foon in an opium den. She sat "on a hank of matting by the side of her opium-soaked mother."

Three-year-old Ho Ping was a slave to a Chinese merchant. He used her as a babysitter. When she could not keep the babies from crying, he tortured her, beating her and burning her with a hot poker. "Three years old!" the writer exclaimed in disbelief. Although rescued and placed in a Christian Chinese home, "Little Ho Ping never lived to laugh and play as all little girls should. Ho Ping died." Illustrations accompanied this article. The artist had interpreted the reporter's words. One drawing shows an angry Chinese man with a whip raised over his head, about to beat a crying child. The drawing wasn't a photograph and so didn't capture a real person about to strike a child. Still, the image was troubling, for it showed abuse.

There were Chinese neighborhoods and mission workers in other cities—Boston, Philadelphia, and Chicago. However, San Francisco was home to the largest number of Chinese immigrants in the United States. The Chinese called San Francisco Dai Fow, or the "Big City." After an earthquake destroyed much of the city and practically all of Chinatown in 1906, the Chinese community rebuilt its neighborhoods. New brick buildings with storefront

In 1900 Helen F. Clark wrote The Lady of the Lily Feet and Other Stories of Chinatown. *This collection of stories was based on her knowledge of the place of women and the general social conditions in America's Chinatowns.*

> Some of the women did not understand the circumstances under which they had been brought to the United States. Once in the country, they discovered a harrowing truth—they were property to be bought and sold as slaves or prostitutes.

windows of plate glass replaced rambling wooden hovels. Chinese American shop owners and business owners, as well as the Chinese middle class, established new organizations to "clean up Chinatown's image." They built schools for their children and hospitals. They published newspapers and established a Chinese Chamber of Commerce. According to the newspaper *Chung Sai Yat Po*, by 1911 Chinese immigrants had begun to wear westernized, or American, clothing. Community leaders had cracked down on gambling and the street gangs known as tongs. They had attempted also to reduce prostitution. Many of these organizations cooperated with Christian-based groups who opened missions in the communities.

Behind this new Chinatown facade, however, was "a ghetto plagued by overcrowding, substandard housing, and poor sanitation." There were few families and significantly more unmarried Chinese men than Chinese women. Many men smuggled women from China into the United States by falsely stating

that these women were their wives. Some of the women did not understand the circumstances under which they had been brought to the United States. Once in the country, they discovered a harrowing truth—they were property to be bought and sold as slaves or prostitutes.

This was the situation for Wong Ah So. In the United States, the man she thought was to be her husband told her he had been paid five hundred dollars to go to China and bring back a woman. "Everybody did this," he told her. "What was so shocking," he asked, "about being a prostitute instead of a married woman?" Apparently, he did not see a difference.

Wong Ah So was alone in a strange land. The only person she knew had betrayed her. She had little choice but to do as commanded. Her new owners, she said, kept close watch over her so she could not escape. She was "very miserable and unhappy." Yet she had a duty to help her mother in China pay her debts. She sent her money to China instead of using it to barter for her own freedom. A missionary worker rescued her a few weeks later and placed her under the protective care of Donaldina Cameron in a mission home.

Donaldina Cameron was a tough moral crusader. She risked her life to rescue thousands of Chinese women who, like Wong Ah So, had been smuggled into the United States. Although she provided a safe haven for these rescued women, she referred to the Chinese as "an alien and heathen people." She portrayed them in condescending ways. The "hateful practice of buying and selling their women like so much merchandise," she said, " . . . is born in their blood, bred in the bone." The rescued women called her *lo mo*, meaning "mother." The angry tongs called her *fan gwai*, meaning "foreign devil." Newspapers praised her as a saint.

Donaldina Cameron became superintendent of the Occidental Mission Home for Girls in 1900. The institution, renamed Cameron House in her honor, is still an important family service organization serving low-income Asian immigrants in the Chinatown area of San Francisco.

These two stories of rescue and racism, one on the East Coast and the other on the West Coast, are typical of the way the media portrayed not only Chinese immigrant women but also the missionaries who worked with them. The sensational language in one story and the derogatory language in the other reflect how many Americans perceived these women.

SATURDAY'S CHILDREN

"I do not know whether I am happy or not," wrote Dorothy Richardson in 1905. She was a working woman. While she daydreamed of other possibilities, she was fairly certain that she would remain a wage earner for the rest of her life. "For I was born on a Saturday," she said, "and 'Saturday's child must work for its living.'"

Richardson was referring to a Mother Goose nursery rhyme, one

Women are shown working in a New England shoe factory in 1910. Most such factories operated six days a week, with twelve-hour workdays beginning at six in the morning.

that helped children learn the days of the week:

> Monday's Child is fair of face.
> Tuesday's Child is full of grace.
> Wednesday's Child is full of woe.
> Thursday's Child has far to go.
> Friday's Child is loving and giving.
> Saturday's Child works hard for a living.
> But the child born on the Sabbath Day
> is bonny and blithe, and good and gay.

Even if Dorothy Richardson had been born on some other day of the week, she would have had to work. Her husband died when she was just eighteen years old, leaving her alone. Richardson lived on a farm in Iowa. She understood that she had to "work or starve." She traveled by train and ferry to New York City, where thousands of single women found work. Richardson hoped to find what might be considered ladylike work rather than immigrant work. Immigrant women worked in factories and sweatshops. They operated pedal-powered sewing machines, stitched artificial flowers, sorted feathers, and rolled tobacco. Immigrants worked with their hands for very low pay. Richardson had only a few dollars to her name, but she wasn't an immigrant. She did not want to work with her hands. Days of disappointment followed, however. Without experience and references, a single woman had difficulty securing a job as a governess or a telephone operator. She did not know how to type. So work with her hands she must. In the months that followed, she worked at a number of temporary jobs—in a box factory; an underwear factory; a laundry; and a large emporium, or store.

In 1905 Dorothy Richardson published a book based on her experiences among the working girls of New York City. She titled the book *The Long Day: The Story of a New York Working Girl, as Told by Herself.* At the time she published the book, Richardson had improved her situation dramatically. She had saved money to go to night school to learn English grammar and other subjects. She succeeded in getting a job on a magazine and had the opportunity to write about her earlier experiences. Either way—whether making boxes and artificial flowers or writing newspaper stories and a book—Richardson was a working girl. All working girls were Saturday's children.

How did society perceive Saturday's children? Some people believed they were wild women adrift in the city. "They work all day and dance all night," *Ladies' Home Journal* stated in an article titled "East Side Girl," in 1899. Many women who worked in factories earned less than $8 a week, though a few earned as much as $12. An employer, however, might subtract a few quarters or more if the worker arrived late. A woman who was ill and did not show up to work earned nothing that day. From these weekly wages, the worker had to pay for food, clothes, and a place to live. Like Richardson, many women lived in boardinghouses. A small room in an attic or in a hallway might cost $1.50 a week. If the room was close to the factory, then the worker did not need to spend money on a trolley or a train. A few extra coins could mean a few hours of cheap amusements. Since most working women rose at five thirty in the morning to start work at seven, dancing all night was unlikely.

> Since most working women rose at five thirty in the morning to start work at seven, dancing all night was unlikely.

THE HELLO GIRLS

Inside a telephone exchange building, the Hello girls were at work. Dozens of women sat on stools in a long row. They faced a wall that looked something like a pegboard with hundreds of outlets and tiny blinking lights. Each operator moved rapidly. When a light flashed, she plugged an electric cord into the outlet. "Number please?" she asked. She then connected the caller to the person being dialed by pulling another electric cord from the base of the machine and plugging it into the right outlet.

At the turn of the century, the telephone was a new and an increasingly important means of communication. The Hello girls, as operators were known, were American-born women. Telephone companies did not hire immigrants. A Hello girl had to speak clearly in English without an accent. Most were high school graduates. In 1910 the Boston Main Exchange had stopped advertising for operators because too many immigrants had applied. In addition to be being illiterate, said the chief operator of the exchange, the immigrants were "untidy" in appearance.

A job with the Boston company paid fairly well—in 1912 five dollars a week as a starting salary was common. The company provided coffee and tea, and even couches where the workers might rest. They each had thirty minutes for lunch. The work, however, was intense. So many calls came through the exchange at once that the operators were constantly pegging and unpegging cords.

Discipline was strict. Floorwalkers moved up and down behind the operators as they worked. Supervisors secretly monitored the Hello girls' responses by listening on "test wires." Despite the coffee, couches, and decent salary, many Hello girls said good-bye to the job after about two years. The hundreds of blinking lights, jumble of electric cords, and floorwalkers who urged them to speed up were just too stressful.

This 1915 photo shows a Hello girl at work. She is one of many young women in the room, each handling about one hundred phone lines and five hundred extensions. Operating the elaborate system was not only high-tech but also high stress.

The beach at Coney Island in New York may not have had the privacy and elegance of polite Society's Newport Beach. But the ocean was just as refreshing and the price was right for working people.

Sadie Frowne earned less than seven dollars a week as a sewing machine operator in a factory in New York City. She was thrifty with her earnings, saving some each week. But she also treated herself to a new hat or another piece of clothing occasionally. "A girl must have clothes if she is to go into high society," she said. High society for young, working immigrants, such as Sadie Frowne, however, was not tea at New York's Waldorf-Astoria Hotel. It was an afternoon at Coney Island amusement park, a ticket to a motion-picture

show, or a few hours at a dance hall. Eight hours of endless pedaling while bent over a sewing machine exhausted Frowne. Work was a necessity, but fashion and fun were necessary too, she insisted. A young woman had to feel good about herself. "You must have some pleasure," said Frowne.

The older women in her neighborhood scolded her for spending one dollar a week on her new clothes. They were from the old country, Frowne said, and had old-fashioned ideas. She was a young and modern American woman. The old country was an old memory to her by then. "People who have been here a long time know better," she said. "A girl who does not dress well is stuck in a corner, even if she is pretty."

Being fashionable wasn't just to attract a man. A woman's self-esteem and her reputation among other women depended, in part, on having style. Often she imitated, as best she could, the styles in the department store windows. In a steamy laundry, Dorothy Richardson noted a young working woman who had bound her hair with a pretty ribbon in the style being displayed "in every shop window in New York." Many immigrant working women would eat only a bit of dry bread for lunch in order to save their nickels to buy a fifty-cent hat. Such a hat wasn't usually much to look at, said one working woman. But the other women always noticed a new hat. In Chicago, social worker Jane Addams watched the working women coming and going from the factories. Addams ran a settlement house for immigrant women. "As these overworked girls stream along the street, the rest of us see only the self-conscious walk, the giggling speech, the preposterous clothing. And yet through the huge hat, with its wilderness of bedraggled feathers, the girl announces to the world that she is here." That their clothing was "preposterous" was, of course, Jane Addams's opinion.

> "And yet through the huge hat, with its wilderness of bedraggled feathers, the girl announces to the world that she is here."
>
> —Dorothy Richardson

Strikebreakers and Suffragists

Immigrant women dominated the workforce in the factories. Some spoke English, but many did not. Within the factory, they communicated with one another using hand gestures. Working conditions were deplorable in some factories. The air was thick with lint. Windows were closed tightly, so no fresh air circulated. The hours were long and the work dangerous, especially in those factories that did not follow safety guidelines. Sewing needles pierced fingers. Hair caught in spinning wheels. According to factory supervisors and owners, these were accidents caused by the workers' carelessness or lack of attention. Many of the factories were firetraps. The crowded rooms and the lack of fire escapes were a catastrophe waiting to happen. And catastrophes did happen. Factory fires and deaths were frequent. Factory owners promised to bring their buildings up to the city's fire codes, but often they did not.

A small group of women who worked in the New York City garment industry organized a series of strikes to protest wage cuts. Within two days, they were joined by twenty to thirty thousand fellow workers, male and female.

In some locations, supervisors locked the doors to stairways so that the workers could not sneak away to rest. They followed them into the lavatory to ensure they didn't waste too much time there, either. At the end of the workday, the women stood in line by the door while supervisors made certain they had not stolen a spool of thread or a yard of ribbon.

The women factory workers demanded better wages and a shorter working day, reduced from ten hours to eight. Some union leaders addressed sexual harassment. Rose Schneiderman confronted a male supervisor on behalf of the women who worked for him. He pinched them as he walked past. The man did not deny it. He did, however, claim no wrongdoing. "Why, Miss Schneiderman," he said, "these girls are like

VOTES for WOMEN.

Unity is strength!

This suffrage poster shows the young sporty girl, the lady of polite Society, the working girl, and the woman with no social status at all. They may have been worlds apart in their day-to-day life, but when it came to women's rights, they were able to join hands over the slogan "Unity is strength!"

my children!" Reportedly, one of the women answered that she'd rather be an orphan.

The women workers became a powerful voice for labor reform. They used the best weapon they had—themselves. They walked out in protest. A strike might last a day or a week, sometimes longer. The women who walked the picket line were often the same immigrants who had arrived in the United States as hopeful young women, eager to start a new life. They were the same women who gazed at the displays in department store windows, who ate lunches that cost just two cents to save a quarter for a new hat. They had learned English. But they were learning something else—if they joined

together, they could be powerful.

The strikers appeared on street corners or paraded in front of closed factory doors. Police arrested them, usually for disturbing the peace and sometimes for assault. The factory owners sometimes hired thugs to beat the strikers into submission. Those violent tactics usually failed. Thugs had broken Clara Lemlich's ribs. A few days later, she returned to the picket line, bruised but more determined than ever to improve the working girl's life through better wages and safer workplaces.

The media images of striking women varied. During a 1902 strike in Boston, the *Globe* newspaper noted that many of the women taking part in the demonstration were "young and remarkably handsome, so that the task of the policeman in driving them away was not altogether an agreeable one, but they did it." Two days later, the same newspaper (though perhaps not the same reporter) called the strikers "shrieking women."

Suffragists joined the cause of working women. Suffrage wasn't just about winning the vote, they told newspapers. It was about treating women humanely, ensuring their work safety, and ensuring their health. Until women got the vote, they argued, employers would continue to take advantage of the working women. Working women called these women of polite Society "the mink brigade." These women referred to the workers as "girls." In part, the word drummed up public sympathy.

The *Boston Herald* quoted a fashionable woman of polite Society who had witnessed the arrests of working women on strike. "One little girl was led away by two officers—imagine a little girl weighing only about 100 or 115 pounds [45 to 52 kg] being taken in charge by two great men!" said a woman who was identified as Mrs. Davis R. Dewey. "The girls were frightened to death—nice girls, who had never seen the inside of a police station before."

The strikers didn't much like that little girl image, said social historian Sarah Deutsch. They endured beatings and broken ribs and still marched the picket line. Though many were young and many were frightened, they were not girls. They "defined themselves as fighters," wrote Deutsch.

FIRE!

The twelve jurors in the courtroom were all men. In 1912 women could not serve on juries, just as they could not vote in elections. The two men on trial were the owners of the Triangle Shirtwaist Factory, housed in New York City. Many months earlier, in March 1911, just minutes before the end of the workday, fire had spread through the eighth, ninth, and tenth floors of the factory. The fire department's ladders did not reach higher than the sixth floor. Many of the factory's workers died within the burning building. Some bodies were burned beyond recognition. The charred remains were carefully placed in coffins marked by numbers only. Others leaped to their deaths from the ninth-floor windows. Although firefighters held nets and blankets to catch them, the force of their tumbling bodies from nine stories above was too great. They tore through the net and onto the pavement.

The ghastly news made headlines in newspapers across the country: 146 people had died, most of them working women, some in their teenage years and others in their twenties and thirties. Most were immigrant women from Italy, Russia, Hungary, and Germany. Even as mourners continued to identify the remains, police and fire investigators began searching for an explanation. A chemical explosion apparently had triggered the fire. Huge piles of fabric trimmings on the floor and in the aisles quickly burst into flame and the fire spread rapidly. Many workers escaped, mostly from the eighth floor, where a single elevator operated. There were so many workers on the eighth floor that the elevator never climbed to the ninth. On this floor, the door to the staircase was locked, stated the survivors, trapping the occupants in the burning building.

When the factory owners appeared in the courtroom, crowds of still grieving relatives shouted, "Murderers! Bring back our children!" The men were not on trial for murder. They had been charged with manslaughter. (Murder is premeditated and planned. Manslaughter is death caused by negligence or intentional recklessness.)

During the trial, fire inspectors and police officers, as well as the workers themselves, testified to what had happened. That the door was locked seemed without a doubt. Whether the two men on trial knew the door was locked was more

Firefighters work to douse the March 25, 1911, fire at the Triangle Shirtwaist Factory at the corner of Greene Street and Washington in New York City.

difficult to prove. The jury returned a verdict of not guilty.

In the days and weeks that followed first the fire and then the trial, indignation and cries for labor reform filled the pages of newspapers. "At last the patience of the people has been exhausted," wrote the director of the American Museum of Safety to the *New York Times*. In fact, the Triangle Shirtwaist Factory was one of hundreds in New York City that failed to meet fire prevention regulations, testified the city's fire chief, John Kenlon.

The tragedy stirred the conscience of many Americans. During a memorial procession through the city to mourn the dead, thousands of working men and women walked solemnly in the rain. They had come not necessarily because they knew the dead. They came because they, too, worked in unsafe conditions. They marched for the victims of the Triangle fire but also for the many thousands of workers killed in the United States each year.

Men and women of middle and upper social classes were also stirred to action. The suffragists who had marched along the picket lines with the strikers a year earlier renewed their support for labor reform. The charred bodies were no longer a nameless group of immigrants. Details about the lives of the dead workers reported in the newspapers in the days following the fire and presented to the jury during the trial months later had succeeded in making society see them as individuals. For the first time, many people understood that the lives of those 146 individuals had value. Frances Perkins was a social worker in New York. She was among those who watched in horror as the building burned and the workers fell to their deaths. She

> During a memorial procession through the city to mourn the dead, thousands of working men and women walked solemnly in the rain. They came because they, too, worked in unsafe conditions.

People and horses draped in black walk in solemn procession in memory of the 146 victims of the 1911 Triangle Shirtwaist Factory fire in New York.

would later attend the memorial service. She herself felt guilty, she said. Everyone in New York City felt that somehow they could not allow such tragedies to continue. Perkins was one of the leaders of a commission assigned to investigate the fire and other workplace-related tragedies. Eventually, New York signed into law new safety restrictions to protect its workers.

Frances Perkins would later explain that "the people of this state saw for the first time the individual worth and value of each of those 146 people who fell or were burned in that great fire. . . . It was the beginning of a new and important drive to bring the humanities to the life of the brothers and sisters we all had in the working groups of these United States."

Chapter Five

In *the* Killing Fields

In my opinion the importance of the part which
our American women must play in the successful
prosecution of the war cannot be overestimated.

—U.S. Navy secretary Joseph Daniels, August 2, 1917

A 1914 drawing shows nurse bandaging
wounded soldier on the battlefield.

American novelist Edith Wharton *was* living *in* Paris

during the summer of 1914. She was enjoying tea with friends one Sunday afternoon in June when someone told them the news. "Haven't you heard? Archduke Ferdinand has been assassinated . . . at Sarajevo." The wife of the archduke had also been "shot dead."

Edith Wharton was a member and an observer of polite Society in such novels as her 1921 Pulitzer Prize–winning book The Age of Innocence. *A strong supporter of the Allied cause in World War I, she wrote reports from the front lines, urging the United States to join the war effort.*

For quite a few moments, a bewildered Edith Wharton tried to piece together the significance of this news. Archduke Franz Ferdinand was the heir to the throne of Austria-Hungary. Sarajevo is a city in Bosnia, a part of Austria-Hungary at the time. The assassin was Serbian. What might the archduke's murder mean for Europe? To avenge the death, might Austria-Hungary declare war on Serbia, with its powerful ally Russia? Austria-Hungary had a strong ally in Germany. Would Germany also go to war?

The news of the assassination would make headlines the next morning in U.S. newspapers. Yet few Americans knew—or cared—about the political consequences of the assassination. Many did not even know where Bosnia was, other than somewhere in the "old country." Americans were more interested in the other news of that summer day: Former U.S. president Theodore Roosevelt was suffering from a fever, and suffragists marched on Washington. In Bar Harbor, Maine, the minister of Sweden and his wife had rented a summer cottage. In Indianapolis, Indiana, a women's medical group debated the benefits and disadvantages of wearing a corset.

In Europe Edith Wharton's fears had come true. Austria-Hungary and Germany declared war on Russia. Russia and its allies, France and Great Britain, in turn declared war on Germany.

Letters *from an* American Nurse *in* France

At the outbreak of war, the daughter of a former medical director of the U.S. Navy was in Paris, France. Her name was never given. She identified herself by the name the soldiers gave her: Mademoiselle Miss. She volunteered "as a helper" in a small French hospital. She studied for her nursing diploma and soon after, the young American woman reported for nursing duties at the front lines of battle.

The letters she wrote home capture some of the horror of war and would later be collected into a book published as *Mademoiselle Miss*. On September 20, 1915, the nurse wrote that she was eager to get started at her job. The wounded began arriving a few days later. By October 2, she wrote that there were so many wounded that she had little free time. And yet, she wrote, "The first time in my life I begin to feel as (a) normal being should, in spite of the blood and anguish in which I move."

October 17, 1915, was an unusual day for the American nurse. No one had died. She referred to herself as a soldier and to the wounded under her care as "her children." Nursing was seen as mothering in the eyes of society, and so it was an acceptable profession for women. Yet no mother buries dozens of children every week as these doctors and nurses had on the front lines.

In other entries, she described a wounded soldier so near death that she called him a living "skeleton." Day after day for weeks, she fed him malted milk and eggs. She bathed him. Changing his bandages took almost two hours. Then one day, she wrote happily, her "skeleton... actually laughed with me and tried to clench his fist inside the dressings to show me how strong he was."

The publication of *Mademoiselle Miss* in Boston in 1916 included photographs of the author in her nurse's uniform. However, her identity remained a mystery. The book became a tool to persuade Americans to contribute money to a fund supporting the wounded in France.

Lines of soldiers await treatment by nurses in a French hospital in January 1914.

By August World War I (1914–1918) had begun. Eventually, those "guns of August" (as the press would later refer to the start of the war) would echo across the Atlantic Ocean and bring the United States into the war.

> As many as twenty-five thousand American women would . . . pack their trunks and head for the front lines.

Edith Wharton could have escaped Paris for Great Britain. She could have returned to the United States. Her friends urged her to go. She could be of greater use in France, she decided. And so she stayed. She volunteered for the Red Cross in France. She would do what she could — raise money for the armies, nurse the wounded, drive an ambulance if needed. She was not alone. As many as twenty-five thousand American women would volunteer. A few, such as Edith Wharton, had been in Europe at the time war exploded. Many more, however, would pack their trunks and board ocean steamships bound for the front lines.

Wanted: Win-the-War Women

Although the United States had remained neutral since August 1914, a number of events would draw the country into the war. These included the 1915 sinking of a British ocean liner, the *Lusitania*, by a German submarine. The death toll was startling — 1,924 people died. Of these, 114 were Americans. The sinking of U.S. ships in 1916 also pushed the United States closer to war. When President Woodrow Wilson at last asked Congress to declare war against Germany, Jeanette Rankin of Montana was the only woman serving in the U.S. House of Representatives. She voted against the war. Rankin was a pacifist, a person who believes in finding peaceful solutions to resolve conflicts. "I am going to Washington to represent the women and children of the West, to work for an eight-hour day for women, and for laws providing that women shall receive the same wages as men for [an] equal amount of work," she stated after winning the election in Montana. She would fight for women's rights, but she would not give her consent for men to die on the battlefields of Europe.

Congress supported President Wilson's declaration of war. The president signed the declaration on April 6, 1917. The government drummed up public support using all means of popular culture and communication—moving pictures, parlor songs, news articles, and posters. The government needed more than men to fight and equipment to fight with—guns, ammunition, and ships. The government also needed women.

In 1917 the president's secretary of the interior outlined the critical role of American women. The war could not be won, stated Franklin K. Lane, unless women understood the moral issues for which Americans were fighting. A patriotic wife supported her husband's decision to

Suffragist and politician Jeanette Rankin, the only woman serving in the U.S. House of Representatives at the time, was one of fifty-seven members to vote against entry into World War I on April 6, 1917. She was a pacifist throughout her life, casting the only House vote against entry into World War II (1939–1945) nearly twenty-five years later.

enlist in the military. A patriotic mother raised her son to fight. A patriotic sister urged her brother to become a soldier.

Women's patriotism extended to the personal letters they wrote to their brothers, sons, husbands, and sweethearts once these men had gone overseas. The letters could be a source of great inspiration. A canteen (military recreation center) worker in Europe shared this story with her family back home: A soldier received a letter from his sister. She wrote that she felt terrible that her brothers had to go to war, but she would "disown them if they didn't." According to the canteen worker, the soldier was "absolutely in a glow with the spirit she had put into him."

A letter from home could have the opposite effect, however, if the woman wrote of her loneliness and fear for her loved one's life. Soldiers agonized over the pain they were causing the women back home. After receiving "a dreadful letter" about his wife's unhappiness, a soldier deserted his duties. The military police found him and placed him under arrest. The penalty for desertion during war was often death by a firing squad. Patriotic wives, mothers, and sisters did not write pessimistic letters.

The military needed women too. It did not want women soldiers. At the turn of the century, the very idea of a female soldier was preposterous. What the military needed, however, was staff to type letters, answer telephones, and perform other office tasks. Approximately eleven thousand women worked for the U.S. Navy as stenographers (typists) and clerks during the war.

Communication was a critical element in war, and telephone operators also joined the military. The government swore into military service approximately two hundred Hello girls and sent them overseas. Their arrival made headlines in the military newspaper *Stars and Stripes*. In addition to speaking clear English, these military Hello girls also had to speak French. Some advanced with the troops to serve just behind the front lines.

On the home front, communities and businesses needed women to take the place of those men who entered military service. Hilda Muhlhauser Richards helped organize the country's female workforce. "Women of the country, like men are patriotic," she said. "They wish to do everything they can to help win the war." She emphasized an important point, however. Women's war work was temporary. Once

The Navy League, a group that supported the men of the marine services and their families, puts out a call for women members in this 1916 poster.

the war ended, women would give up their jobs to the returning veterans. A good many people believed women could not do the same work that men had done or at least not as well. Hiring women to fill vacancies in the workforce was a wartime experiment. Yet someone had to operate the streetcars and elevators, deliver the mail, and police the streets. In the spring of 1918, in New York City alone, there were reportedly more than six hundred vacancies on the police force.

On a December morning in 1917, the post office in New York City sent out ten women on a trial basis. They delivered the mail on time and without any apparent incident. Within weeks more female letter carriers were delivering sacks of mail. They didn't carry packages or heavy boxes, however. Lifting heavy objects was part of a postman's job, but not a postwoman's.

Prior to the war, much of society had believed women were the weaker sex. Popular culture had both supported that belief and challenged it. After the war began, the government went to work carefully constructing new messages and images to persuade its female citizens—whether housewives or career women, young or old—to answer the call.

In a symbolic gesture, a suffragist poses in a police uniform to promote the idea of women joining the force.

Posters, Parlor Songs, *and* Female Patriotism

The posters appeared in shop windows, post offices, train stations, and theaters. The country's leading graphic artists—Charles Gibson, Howard Christy, and Nell Brinkley—created patriotic images to persuade

Gone is the upswept hair and the pinched-waist figure. Charles Dana Gibson turned his attention to more serious pursuits, as in this 1918 recruitment poster showing a uniformed young woman saluting and checking in for duty with Uncle Sam.

In his version of a recruitment poster, James Flagg chose to portray a woman asleep while the war raged on behind her. Though the message is insulting to women, the poster was very popular and is still distributed in reprint version.

Americans to support the war. Artist James Flagg created perhaps the most famous and lasting image of the war. Flagg portrayed the United States as "Uncle Sam," an older man with white hair and a beard who wore a top hat and a suit of red, white, and blue. His eyes and his pointed finger were directed right toward the viewer. "I want you for the U.S. Army," the text read.

Flagg also created another image of the United States. She was a woman, asleep in a wicker chair while war waged behind her. Her clothing was red, white, and blue. She appeared swathed in a U.S. flag. "Wake up

This 1917 poster (left) *appeals directly to working women, offering the opportunity of nobility in service to her country. Sheet music publishers joined the effort to recruit nurses. This 1918 song* (above) *tells the story of how little Mary Brown finally made something of herself by becoming a nurse.*

America!" the text read, "Civilization calls every man, woman and child!"

Some posters recruited men into military service and women into service as Red Cross nurses or volunteers. The images of women were idealized on these posters. The messages were emotional. "Woman, your country needs you," was the text of a poster that showed a woman warrior. She was dressed as a Greek goddess in a flowing robe. She held a shield and a large sword on which is printed the word *service*. Standing before her was a smaller ordinary-looking woman in plain clothing. She was a working woman rather than a fashionable woman, judging by her hair and her simple dress. She, too, had her hand of the hilt of the sword. The women were noble and proud. The image was representative of many created during the war and meant to appeal to women.

Popular songs and sheet music covers also portrayed noble, self-sacrificing women "doing their bit." The song "The Little Good for Nothing's Good for Something After All" told a story of Mary Brown. She used to be a tomboy, the lyrics stated. During the war, however, she proved herself to be an angel of mercy as a Red Cross volunteer. The image on the sheet music cover showed a woman wearing the Red Cross uniform, with a long cape over her shoulders.

The images of war promoted by the U.S. government communicated a simple message about gender: Men are heroic. Women are angels of mercy. They wore Red Cross caps and starched white uniforms. Often they stood with open arms, reaching out to comfort the country. The images also suggested that angels of mercy were white. Few women of color appeared in government posters or on sheet music illustrations.

The war required huge numbers of nurses, and many recruitment posters targeted them. A Red Cross nurse (above) was usually an angelic-looking woman, dressed in white, offering loving care to stricken soldiers.

Angels *of* Mercy

Nursing was an acceptable women's profession in 1917. However, most nurses worked in community hospitals, not in the military. When the United States entered the war that year, the U.S. Navy had only 160 nurses on active duty. Recruitment of nurses for the navy and the army was critical. Louisa Lee Schuyler was the founder of the Bellevue School of Nursing, the first school to train professional nurses. In a letter to the *New York Times*, she urged qualified nurses to volunteer to enlist in the army and navy nursing corps. "[A nurse] could have no prouder distinction, no greater privilege than to be in this service," Schuyler stated.

Wartime Fashions *and* Femininity

Women were working as never before—in the home, at wartime jobs, at the office, in the factory, and on the farm. The media applauded the women who were doing their bit for the war effort. Yet the media also reminded them that war work should not mean losing their femininity. An advertisement for a face cream appeared in the November 1917 issue of the *Modern Priscilla*. It stated: "Do not forget that there is a duty due yourself and those who care for you. The duty is to hold your youth and beauty in these trying days which bring worn looks and lines of age. To counteract the effects of work and worry and winter winds, get more sleep and form the habit of nightly use of Pompeian Night Cream."

There was also the troubling problem of fashion. If women must wear uniforms, let the uniform at least be attractive, lamented one newspaper reporter. Many public service jobs, such as letter carrier or streetcar conductor, required women to wear uniforms of fitted jackets and trousers. These uniforms were tailored like men's clothing. The blouses buttoned to the neck and were often worn with a tie. The uniform for female conductors of railway cars was a khaki coat that came to the knees and knickerbockers. She often wore knee-high leather boots.

Of course, women who worked on the farm didn't have an official uniform. Most often the "farmerettes," as these women were often called, donned men's bib overalls, heavy shoes, and straw hats.

Women serving as nurses or canteen workers wore military uniforms especially designed for them. In a letter home, an

Pompeian Night Cream, as advertised in the Modern Priscilla *in 1917, is shown erasing the signs of wartime stress from a woman's face.*

This wartime postcard is appealing but not totally honest. It shows a happy uniformed nurse with Gibson-style upswept hair, a tiny waist, and shirtwaist blouse of the era. Life in army hospitals, however, was not as lovely as the postcard implies.

American canteen volunteer working in France summed up her feelings about wartime fashions. She wrote: "For eighteen months I haven't worn white gloves, or silk stockings, or a veil, no, nor even powdered my nose. And the worst of it is, these things don't seem to matter any more."

One nurse, in writing home, complained that soldiers thought the women ugly in their rain hats and raincoats and rubber boots. How she looked, however, wasn't as important as staying dry and warm. When given a chance to go shopping, she spent her money on a warm knit undershirt rather than a lacy blouse or ribboned hat.

Not all women shared the canteen worker's point of view. A homesick ambulance driver wrote to her friend in Great Britain about her hut near the front lines. She was huddling close to a smelly oil stove and still freezing to death. Khaki uniforms were "superghastly," she wrote. She longed to wear again a soft crepe de Chine blouse rather than her military uniform and tie. Gladys de Havilland had a name for such women. In *The Woman's Motor Manual*, a guidebook on driving motorcars in the military, she called them "butterfly chauffeusses (female chauffeurs)." The butterflies, she noted, usually didn't last long. To succeed as an ambulance driver, a woman had to stop thinking of herself as a pampered pet.

But Schuyler reminded women of the cost that could come from such unselfish service. She wrote:

> [The military nurse] may be called upon to give life and health as her brothers in the army and the navy are doing and have done. She may be torpedoed at sea, or bombed on land; for we are dealing with an enemy who knows no respect for the Red Cross flag.

Recruitment of nurses and Red Cross workers ignored women of color. Even when African American nurses by the thousands volunteered to serve in hospitals overseas, the government refused to accept them. The nurses chosen were white. Likewise, the American Red Cross chose not to accept women of color. This decision reflected a racial divide that existed in many U.S. communities. The races did not live or work side by side as equals. Not even war would change that form of racism.

Addie Waites Hunton, however, persevered in her efforts to have the Young Men's Christian Association (YMCA) send her overseas to work with the African American troops. Although there were approximately two hundred thousand African American troops, Hunton was one of only three American women of color to serve with the American troops in Europe during the war. Because the military was segregated, she and the other two women—Kathryn Johnson and Helen Curtis—were also segregated. They taught the soldiers how to read and write, showed newsreels and movies, gave lectures, and generally helped to boost their morale.

FIVE THOUSAND BY JUNE

GRADUATE NURSES YOUR COUNTRY NEEDS YOU

The U.S. government called for five thousand nurses by June of 1917. Women answered the call. Eventually the Army Nursing Corps swelled to about twenty-two thousand with another fourteen hundred serving in the Navy Nursing Corps.

Women *and the* Influenza Pandemic *of* 1918

The army, navy and the Red Cross had recruited thousands of nurses for military service during the war. While the country understood that medical staff was needed "over there" on the battlefields of Europe, another war was about to erupt and spread across the United States. The shortage of doctors and nurses would make the casualties of this war even greater than the hundreds of thousands dying in the trenches.

Nurses care for victims of influenza in outdoor facilities in Lawrence, Massachusetts, in 1918.

Between 1918 and 1919, influenza would kill 20 million people around the world, compared to World War I's toll of 10 million.

The outbreaks of sickness happened first on army bases where soldiers trained for being shipped overseas. The symptoms were: bleeding from the nose and ears, sometimes the eyes; coughing so violently that abdominal muscles tore; muscle pains and confusion or hallucinations. Some vomited. The skin turned blue, at first around the lips or fingertips. In the fatal cases—and there would be so many cities that could not bury their dead—the body turned a deep blue, almost black.

Newspaper headlines reported the number of dead, often one thousand or more in a single day. One of the worst days of the pandemic in Philadelphia was October 16, 1918. More than forty-five hundred people died from influenza.

Newspaper headlines also appealed for nurses to report for duty. But there were just too few nurses to answer the call. Those doctors and nurses who aided the sick themselves became ill, and many died. Young nursing students in their third or fourth year of college left the classroom to work in the hospitals and community clinics.

In Philadelphia, as in other cities across the country, women stepped forward to do what they could. They organized soup kitchens to feed the children of parents who were ill or had died. They operated telephone banks to answer the thousands of calls for help. They provided cars for ambulances to carry the sick to the hospitals or other emergency clinics set up in schools and other public buildings. They cut and sewed gauze masks and distributed them throughout the community. American women were strong and resourceful.

What was life like for a nurse overseas during World War I? The war posters and parlor songs promoted the glory of service but suggested nothing of the reality of war. Many newspaper articles praised nurses but failed to mention the often harsh conditions of the camps or the grimness of war wounds and disease. The nurses' letters to family back home painted a fuller picture. While some nurses worked in resort hotels converted to hospitals, many worked in field tents. Running water was not always available. Daisy Urch wrote of a storm at a camp near the English Channel that "threatened to blow the entire hospital into the sea."

Dampness and crowding within the medical base camps exposed nurses to diseases such as typhus, influenza, scarlet fever, and measles. Nurses close to the battlefield tended to wounds and amputations. An important task was cleaning the raw wounds of all debris, such as dirt and gravel. They cut away infected tissue and irrigated, or washed, the wounds. Julia Stimson was the chief nurse of the American Expeditionary Forces. She reported that nurses often spent as many as fourteen hours in the operating room. The odors of ether (a gas used to anesthetize soldiers during an operation), blood, and infected wounds made the nurses and physicians sick to their stomachs. After the war, she would describe a vivid scene of wartime nursing involving a man in his hospital cot, "dying of burns." It was, she said, "a revolting sight." Yet sitting beside him and holding his hand was a nurse.

Enlisted men who worked in medical camps might refuse to take orders from a woman, even a nurse in charge of a hospital unit. A nurse did not have a military rank, they reasoned.

Helen Fairchild worked in an operating hospital close to the fighting in France. Nurses working close to the front lines were sometimes the victims of mustard gas, a type of chemical used during the war. It caused painful blistering of the body, including the eyes, nose, and throat. In January 1918, the U.S. War Department wrote to Fairchild's family with the sad news that their daughter had died while on duty. Although the letter did not explain the cause of her death, she had been exposed to poisonous mustard gas. The family would later learn that Nurse Fairchild had at least on one occasion given her own gas mask to a wounded soldier for his protection.

Missing, too, from the war propaganda and news articles about the American Expeditionary Forces was the tension between nurses and the military staff. Enlisted men who worked in medical camps might refuse to take orders from a woman, even a nurse in charge of a hospital unit. A nurse did not have a military rank, they reasoned. They were not officers. Physicians, too, often questioned nurses' medical training or resented nurses who suggested certain treatments.

Nurses such as the one Julia Stimson described caring for the soldier dying of burns were indeed "angels of mercy." But they were also trained professionals who suffered the same war traumas as many of the soldiers. The popular media applauded its women war heroines, but it often did not understand what their war experiences were.

Suffragists picket in front of the White House in February 1917. They believed that voting was an issue of liberty and justice, the same values that were at stake during the war.

The Silent Sentinels

Not even a world war would defer the suffragists. While Americans fought overseas on the battlefields of France, the struggle for women's rights continued. Before the United States entered the war, Alice Paul and members of the National Woman's Party made a controversial decision. Like the militant suffragettes in Great Britain, they believed the time had come to agitate political leaders into action for an amendment to the Constitution. The position of greatest power in government was the presidency. No organization before had picketed the White House. These women would be the first. They called themselves the silent sentinels.

The protest began in January 1917. The sentinels came armed with purple and gold flags and with placards that read, "Mr. President, how long must women wait for liberty?" And "Democracy should begin at home." The silent sentinels were not alone. Often spectators gathered. People opposed to suffrage came as well. They heckled and ridiculed the suffragists. Throughout winter and spring, the picketing continued.

The banners the silent sentinels displayed became more controversial during the war. Statements accused the president of being a hypocrite—sending U.S. troops to fight for freedom in Europe while American women were not free. Printed across a 10-foot-wide (3 m) banner were these words: "We, the women of America, tell you that America is not a democracy. Twenty million American women are denied the right to vote." A crowd of angry men tore the banner from the suffragists, the *New York Times* reported. Women spectators, too, were furious that the suffragists had used the phrase

"We, the women of America, tell you that America is not a democracy. Twenty million American women are denied the right to vote."

—suffragist banner, 1917

"We, the women of America." The suffragists did not speak for them, some women said. The suffragists—some sneeringly called them "suffergets"—were unpatriotic.

For months the president and his administration largely ignored the silent sentinels who appeared daily on the sidewalk in front of the White House. But they were becoming more troublesome. The antisuffragists, too, were more enraged. Conflicts were daily occurrences. Then the arrests began. The police charged the suffragists with blocking street traffic. The next day, however, other suffragists had taken the place of those who had been arrested. In fact, suffragists from other states were coming to the nation's capital to take their turn as silent sentinels. The arrests continued. A judge fined the women, and when they refused to pay the fines, the police placed them in the Occoquan Workhouse, a prison across the Potomac River in Virginia. While in prison, many women refused to eat. Doctors force-fed them. Some women were beaten. In November 1917, President Wilson ordered the release of the suffragists in the Occoquan Workhouse. The government would later rule that the arrests of the silent sentinels had been illegal.

Meanwhile, another force of suffragists was also at work. A delegation of women who worked in an ammunitions plant in New Castle, Pennsylvania, traveled to Washington to meet with President Wilson. Women were helping the United States win the war by doing men's work—in factories, on railroads, in lumberyards, in offices, and in government departments such as the post office. The time had come to recognize women's worth.

The treatment of the wartime suffragists was harsh. Here a jailed picketer who has refused to eat is being force-fed.

t epilogue
the tolling of the bells, 1918

*t*he war was over, and we thought we were returning to the world we had so abruptly passed out of four years earlier. Perhaps it was as well that, at first, we were sustained by that illusion.

—Edith Wharton, A *Backward Glance* (1934)

Illustration showing troops being welcomed home, cover of St. Nicholas magazine, 1918

On a "hushed November day" in 1918,

Edith Wharton heard an unexpected sound. Somewhere outside the city of Paris, a church bell was ringing. For four years, she had become accustomed to the sounds of war—air-raid siren wailings, guns firing, and bombs exploding. Church bells had also rung, but not at this "unusual hour," she said. She stepped out onto the balcony and listened.

She heard not one bell but another and then another, as if they were calling across the city. At first, the calling was soft, but then it increased in volume. More bells were tolling, she realized. "Their voices met and mingled in a crash of triumph," she would later write. "We had fared so long on the thin diet of hope deferred that for a moment or two our hearts wavered and doubted," she wrote. "Then, like the bells, they swelled to bursting, and we knew the war was over."

"their voices met and mingled in a crash of triumph."

—Edith Wharton, *A Backward Glance* (1934)

Later, as she watched the Allied forces (soldiers, including those from the United States, who fought against Germany and its allies) march victorious into Paris, she felt happy that at last there would be no more killing fields. But soon that happiness faded, and sorrow took its place. It had been a dark four years. She mourned for all who had been lost. She felt as if her heart had broken.

Just as a century does not end in a single moment, nor does a war. A door had not slammed shut with the surrender of the German ruler and his forces in 1918. Rather, a window opened, and change, like wind, rifled through the curtains, hinting of what might come.

Many soldiers returned home with wounds. Even those who were whole physically carried with them scarring memories of what they had seen. War had challenged and changed women too. Many removed Red Cross caps and aprons. They untied and tossed aside, at least for a while, their medical masks of gauze. They gave up their jobs in the factories, and they returned home. "We thought we were returning to the world we had so abruptly passed out of four years earlier," wrote Edith Wharton. But that world had changed, and life would never quite be the same again.

One significant change occurred in the last weeks of the war. For two years, suffragists had pressured President Wilson to take a stand on woman suffrage. On September 20, 1918, he finally did. He addressed the Senate, firmly stating his support for the Nineteenth Amendment, which would give women the right to vote.

Women's unselfish contributions during the war, in particular, were evidence of their ability to serve their country. "This war could not have been fought," he stated, " . . . if it had not been for the services of the women . . . rendered in every sphere—not merely in the fields of effort in which we have been accustomed to see them work but wherever men have worked and upon the very skirts and edges of the battle itself." He asked, "Shall we admit them only to a partnership of sacrifice and suffering and toil and not to a partnership of privilege and of right?"

It had been a long, hard battle, but suffragists won the right to vote when the Nineteenth Amendment to the U.S. Constitution became law in 1920.

If there had never been a war or if the United States had never entered the war, would Congress have passed the Nineteenth Amendment in 1920 giving women the right to vote? Perhaps, for other social events and changes occurred throughout the nineteenth and early twentieth centuries that altered what society believed about women. From "true womanhood" to Gibson girl, from Gibson girl to the athletic Fisher girl and the working girls of the factory, from bawdy women of the stage and screen to suffragists—women's roles in society were changing. Popular culture, too, would continue to reflect these changes.

Source Notes

6   David F. Burg, *Chicago's White City of 1892* (Lexington: University Press of Kentucky, 1976), 104.

9   Hubert Howe Bancroft, *The Book of the Fair* (Chicago: Bancroft Company, 1893), 267.

12 Bertha Honoré Potter Palmer, "Opening Address," in *The Congress of Women: Held in the Woman's Building, World's Columbian Exposition*, edited by Mary Kavanaugh Oldham Eagle (Chicago: Monarch Book Company, 1894), 25.

12 Ibid, 26.

12 Ibid, 27.

12 Ibid, 28.

13 Ibid, 29.

14 Edward Marshall, "The Gibson Girl Analyzed by Creator," *New York Times*, November 20, 1910, SM6.

15 Lloyd Morris, *Postscript to Yesterday: America—the Last Fifty Years* (New York: Random House, 1947), 4.

16 Ibid., 7.

16 Bryan Holme and Katharine Tweed, eds., *The World in Vogue* (New York: Viking Press, 1963), 43.

17 *New York Times*, "What Is Doing in Society," July 30, 1899, 12.

18 Ibid.

18–19 *New York Times*, "Newport Society at Vanderbilt Dance," July 30, 1904, 7.

19–20 Kay Davis, "Class and Leisure at America's First Resort Newport, Rhode Island, 1870–1914" (master's thesis, University of Virginia, 2001), available online at http://xroads.virginia.edu/~ma01/davis/newport/home/home.html (February 10, 2007).

21 "Newport Society at Vanderbilt Dance."

21 *New York Times*, "Mrs. McMemomin Hurt?" July 14, 1904, 7.

21 Ibid.

23 Morris, 9.

23–24 Barbara Belford, *Brilliant Bylines: A Biographical Anthology of Notable Newspaperwomen in America* (New York: Columbia University Press, 1986), 77.

26–25 Desley Deacon, *Elsie Clews Parsons: Inventing Modern Life*. (Chicago: University of Chicago Press, 1997), 68–69.

26 Margaret Sanger, *An Autobiography* (New York: W. W. Norton, 1938), 77.

28 Project Gutenberg, "The Young Housewife's Latest," *Good Stories from the Ladies' Home Journal, Project Gutenberg*, July 7, 2004, http://www.gutenberg.org/etext/12836 (February 1, 2007).

32 *New York Times*, "Gibson Girl's Creator and American Girl Types," June 20, 1905, SM4.

32 *New York Times*, "The Gibson Girl Analyzed by Her Originator," November 20, 1910, SM6.

33 Time Life Books, *This Fabulous Century*, vol. 2, (New York: Time Life Books, 1969), 111.

35 M. Carey Thomas, "The Passionate Desire of Women . . . for Higher Education," in *Women's America: Refocusing the Past*, edited by Linda K. Kerber and Jane Sherron De Hart (New York: Oxford University Press, 1995), 273–275.

36 Trina Robbins, "The Day of the Girl: Nell Brinkley and the New Woman," in *New Woman Hybridities: Femininity, Feminism and International Consumer Culture, 1880–1930*, edited by Margaret Beetham and Ann Heilmann (New York: Routledge, 2004), 181.

36 Ibid.

37 Ibid., 183.

37 Ibid.

38 Carolyn Kitch, *The Girl on the Magazine Cover: The Origins of Visual Stereotypes in American Mass Media* (Chapel Hill: University of North Carolina Press, 2001) 95.

38 Ibid.

38 Morris, 21.

39 Alice Sheppard, *Cartooning for Suffrage* (Albuquerque: University of New Mexico Press, 1994), 22.

40 Zitkala-Sa, *American Indian Stories* (Lincoln: University of Nebraska Press, 1985), viii.

40 Ibid., 8.

41 *New York Times*, "Calls Women Cowards," July 28, 1912, 11.

41 Ibid.

43 *New York Times*, "Women Revealed as Heroines by Wreck," April 20, 1912, 4.

43 Ibid.

44 Gail Collins. *America's Women: 400 Years of Dolls, Drudges, Helpmates and Heroines* (New York: Harper Collins, 2003) 2.

44–45 Elizabeth Smith Miller and Anne Fitzhugh Miller, "Miller NAWSA Suffrage Scrapbooks, 1897–1911," *Library of Congress American Memory*, n.d., http://memory.loc.gov/cgi-bin/query/r?ammem/rbcmillerbib:@field(DOCID+@lit(rbcmiller002114) (June 7, 2007).

46 *New York Times*, "Women Here and There—Her Frills and Fancies," September 23, 1900, 19.

47 Department of Agriculture,"How the U.S. Department of Agriculture Can Better Meet the Needs of Farm Housewives" (Washington, D.C.: Government Printing Office, 1915), 55.

47 Mark Sullivan and Dan Rather, eds. *Our Times: American at the Birth of the 20th Century* (New York: Scribner, 1996), 31–32.

48 Philip Scranton, ed., *Beauty and Business* (New York: Routledge, 2001), 37.

49 Sullivan and Rather, 395.

50 Curt McConnell, *A Reliable Car and a Woman Who Knows It: The First Coast-to-Coast Auto Trips by Women, 1899–1916* (Jefferson, NC: McFarland Publishers, 2000), 1.

50 Ibid., 25.

50 *New York Times*, "Her Own Mechanic on Drive to 'Frisco,'" June 6, 1909, S4.

51 McConnell, 23.

54–55 R. A. Adams, *The Social Dance* (Kansas City, KS: privately published, 1921), 8.

55 Ibid., 14.

56 *New York Times*, "Social Workers See Real 'Turkey Trots,'" January 27, 1912, 1.

58 Teresa Riordan, *Inventing Beauty* (New York: Broadway Books, 2004), 137.

59 Senda Berenson, Spaulding's Athletic Library, *Basketball for Women* (New York: American Sports Pub. Co., 1905), 33.

60 *New York Times*, "Girl Athletes Rough It," February 11, 1905, 10.

60 Ibid.

61 Ibid., 68.

63 *New York Times*, "Women Parade and Rejoice at the End," May 7, 1911, 1.

64 Wisconsin Historical Society, "The Anti Woman's Suffrage Poster," *Wisconsin Historical Society*, n.d., http://www.wisconsinhistory.org/whi/fullRecord.asp ?id=1932 (February 10, 2007).

66 Alice Duer Miller, *Are Women People?* (New York: George H. Doran, 1915), 16.

66 Ibid.

66 Ibid.

66 Ellen Carol Dubois, "Working Women, Class Relations and Suffrage Militance," in *Unequal Sisters: A Multicultural Reader in U.S. Women's History*, edited by Ellen Carol DuBois and Vicki L. Riuz (New York: Routledge, 1990), 189.

66 Ibid.

67 Ibid.

69 Ibid.

70 Andrew L. Erdman, *Blue Vaudeville: Sex, Morals and the Mass Marketing of Amusement, 1895–1915* (Jefferson, NC: McFarland & Company, 2004), 146.

72 Ibid., 2.

72 *New York Times*, "Vaudeville a Great Field for Women Says Albee," March 15, 1914, X12.

72–73 Ibid.

74 M. Alison Kibler, *Rank Ladies: Gender and Cultural Hierarchy in American Vaudeville* (Chapel Hill: University of North Carolina Press, 1999), 143.

74 Ibid., 1.

74 Ibid., 2.

75 "Eva Tanguay Is Modest," *New York Times*, March 25, 1913, 8.

75 "Eva Tanguay, the 'I Don't Care Girl,'" *tribe.net*, n.d., http://maewest.tribe.net/thread/7e5726a2-0fce-45d3-96b9-2ed00a08acb7 (June 7, 2007).

76 June Sochen, *Enduring Values: Women in Popular Cultures* (Westport, CT: Praeger, 1987), 64.

79 Linda Mizejewski, *Ziegfeld Girl: Image and Icon in Culture and Cinema* (Durham, NC: Duke University Press, 1999), 13.

80 Eve Golden, *Anna Held and the Birth of Ziegfeld's Broadway* (Lexington: University of Kentucky Press, 2000), 127.

81 *New York Times*, "Mlle. Anna Held Arrives," September 15, 1896, 5.

81 Joyce E. Eberly, "Florenz Ziegfeld," *Suite 101.com*, November 23, 2001, http://www.suite101.com/article .cfm/live_and_on_stage/82684 (June 7, 2007).

82 Mizejewski, 3.

83 Steven Ross, *Movies and American Society* (Malden, MA: Blackwell Publishers, 2002), 17.

83 Ibid., 2.

83–84 Ibid.

84 Ibid., 40.

84 Jeanine Basinger, *Silent Stars* (Hanover, NH: Wesleyan University Press, 1999), 11.

84 *New York Times*, "The Silent Star Speaks," November 18, 1915, X9.

86 Wilson Web, "Lillian Gish," *Current Biography* (New York: H. W. Wilson Company, 1944), n.d., http://vnweb.hwwilsonweb.com/hww/shared/shared_ main.jhtml?_requestid=151500 (February 10, 2007).

86 Ibid.

87 Seymour Peck, "Then and Now: Lillian Gish," *New York Times*, April 17, 1960, SM70.

87 *New York Times*, "Theda Bara Films Test Plot Writers," January 24, 1916, 12.

90 Dorothy Richardson, *The Long Day: The Story of a New York Working Girl, as Told by Herself* (New York: Century Co., 1905), available online in Open Collections Program, "Working Women, 1800–1930, *Harvard University Library*, February 8, 2006, http://pds.harvard.edu:8080/pdx/servlet/pds?op=f&id= 2597696&n=18 (March 7, 2007).

91 Time Life Books, *This Fabulous Century*, vol. 2, 76.

91 Ibid.

91 Ibid.

92 Donna Gabaccia, *Seeking Common Ground: Multidisciplinary Studies of Immigrant Women in the United States* (Westport, CT: Praeger, 1992), 67, 75.

92 Ibid., 79.

92 Ibid

92 Ibid.

93 Ibid., 76.

95 *New York Times*, "Chicago's Chinatown in Danger," May 30, 1900, 2.

95 George J. Sanchez, "'Go After the Women': Americanization and the Mexican Immigrant Woman, 1915–1929," in *Unequal Sisters: A Multicultural Reader in U.S. Women's History*, edited by Ellen Carol DuBois and Vicki L. Ruiz (New York: Routledge, 1990), 253.

96 Jacob A. Riis, *How the Other Half Lives* (New York: Dover Publications, 1971), 91.

96 Ibid.

96 Ibid., 122.

97 Sanchez, 250.

99 Pearl Idelia Ellis, *Americanization through Homemaking* (Los Angeles: Wetzel Publishing Co., 1929), 61.

99 *New York Times*, "Rescuing Angel of the Little Slaves of Chinatown," April 30, 1905, part 4, second magazine section, X4.

99–100 Ibid.

100 Ibid.

101 Judy Yung, *Unbound Feet: A Social History of Chinese Women in San Francisco* (Berkeley: University of California Press, 1995), 68–69.

101 Ibid., 68.

101 Ibid., 70.

102 Laurene Wu Mcclain, "Donaldina Cameron," *Chinese America: History and Perspectives*, no. 26 (San Francisco: Chinese Historical Society, 2001, available online at *Questia*, n.d., http://www.questia.com/PM.qst;jsessionid =FqGTW57gLj1yZp1s6SyST6sC37hbKM0FWTQ LpZq27Q7kJpqDmcJG!226482133?a=o&d=500097 5289 (February 10, 2007).

102 Yung, 73.

102 Richardson, 282.

104 Lois W. Banner, *American Beauty: A Social History through Two Centuries of the American Idea, Ideal, and Image of the Beautiful Woman* (New York: Alfred A. Knopf, 1983), 197.

105 Sarah Deutsh, *Women and the City: Gender, Space and Power in Boston, 1870–1940* (New York: Oxford University Press, 2000), 191.

106 Sadie Frowne, "Days and Dreams," March 2, 2002, reprinted in Leon Stein, ed., *Out of the Sweatshop: The Struggle for Industrial Democracy* (New York: Quadrangle/New Times Book Company, 1977), 60–61, available online at *Cornell University*, 2002, http://www.ilr.cornell.edu/trianglefire/texts/stein _ootss/ootss_sf.html (February 10, 2007).

107 Ibid.

107 Richardson, 232.

107 Jane Addams, *The Spirit of Youth and City Streets*, available online at *Project Gutenberg*, n.d., http://www.gutenberg.org/etext/16221 (February 1, 2007).

108–109 Theresa S. Makiel, *The Diary of a Shirtwaist Striker.* (Ithaca, NY: ILP Press, 1990), 18.

110 Deutsch, 198.

110 Ibid., 199.

110 Ibid., 201.

112 W. H. Tolman, "Startled by City's Dangers," *New York Times*, April 11, 1911, 10.

113 Doug Linder, "Triangle Shirtwaist Factory Fire," *Triangle Shirtwaist Factory Fire*, n.d., http://www.law.umkc.edu/faculty/projects/ftrials/ triangle/triangleaccount.html (February 10, 2007).

114 Ida Clyde Clarke, *American Women and the World War* (New York: Appleton, 1918), available online at *World War I Document Archive, Brigham Young University*, January 2007, http://net.lib.byu.edu/ ~rdh7/wwi/comment/Clarke/Clarke01.htm (March 7, 2007).

115 Edith Wharton, *A Backward Glance* (New York: D. Appleton-Century Co., 1934), 336.

116 Anonymous, *Mademoiselle Miss* (Boston: W. A. Butterfield, 1916), available online at "Women Working 1800–1930," *Harvard University Open Collection Program*, n.d., http://pds.harvard.edu :8080/pdx/servlet/pds?id=2575217 (February 10, 2007), 18.

116 Ibid., 47.

117–118 *New York Times*, "Equal Pay for Women," November 12, 1916, 4.

118 Sullivan and Rather, 559.

118–119 Ibid.

119 Ibid.

119 *New York Times Magazine*, "Woman Now Directs Nation's Women Workers," February 8, 1918, 56.

125 Katharine D. Morse, *Uncensored Letters of a Canteen Girl* (New York: Henry Holt, 1920), available online at *History Matters*, n.d., http://historymatters.gmu.edu/d/5329 (February 10, 2007).

123 U.S. Navy, "Nurses and the U.S. Navy, 1917–1919," *Navy Historical Center*, n.d., http://www.history.navy.mil/index.html (December 16, 2006).

123 *New York Times*, "The Need for Nurses," August 13, 1918, 8.

124 Ibid.

128 Kimberly Jensen, "A Base Hospital Is Not a Coney Island Dance Hall: American Nurses, Hostile Work Environment, and Military Rank in the First World War," *Frontiers, a Journal of Women's Studies* 26, available online at *Questia*, 2005. http://www.questia.com/PM.qst?a=o&d=5012184437 (February 10, 2007).

128 Susan Zeiger, *In Uncle Sam's Service: Women Workers with the American Expeditionary Force, 1917–1919* (Ithaca, NY: Cornell University Press, 1999), 11.

132 Wharton, 362.

133 Ibid., 359–360.

134 Zeiger, 137.

Selected Bibliography

Adams, R. A. *The Social Dance*. Kansas City, KS: Privately published, 1921.

Allen, Frederick Lewis. *The Big Change*. New York: Harper and Brothers, 1952.

Bancroft, Hubert Howe. *The Book of the Fair*. Chicago: Bancroft Company, 1893.

Banner, Lois W. *American Beauty: A Social History through Two Centuries of the American Idea, Ideal, and Image of the Beautiful Woman*. New York: Alfred A. Knopf, 1983.

Barry, John M. *The Great Influenza: The Story of the Deadliest Pandemic in History*. New York: Penguin Books, 2004.

Basinger, Jeanine. *Silent Stars*. Hanover, NH: Wesleyan University Press, 1999.

Belford, Barbara. *Brilliant Bylines: A Biographical Anthology of Notable Newspaperwomen in America*. New York: Columbia University Press, 1986.

Billings, Molly. "Influenza Epidemic of 1918." *Stanford University*, February 2005, http://www.stanford.edu/group/virus/uda (February 10, 2007).

Bureau of Indian Affairs. *Tentative Course of Study for United States Indian Schools*. Washington, DC: Government Printing Office, 1915.

Cardinal, Agnes, Dorothy Goldman, and Judith Hathaway. *Women's Writing on the First World War*. New York: Oxford University Press, 1999.

Castle, Vernon, and Irene Castle. *Modern Dancing*. New York: World Syndicate Co., 1914.

Cunningham, Patricia A. *Reforming Women's Fashion, 1850–1920: Politics, Health, and Art*. Kent, OH: Kent State University Press, 2003.

Deacon, Desley. *Elsie Clews Parsons: Inventing Modern Life*. Chicago: University of Chicago Press, 1997.

Deutsch, Sarah. *Women and the City: Gender, Space and Power in Boston, 1870–1940*. New York: Oxford University Press, 2000.

Dewey, Vivian Persis. *Tips for Dancers: Good Manners for Ballroom and Dance Hall*. Kenosha, WI: Privately published, 1918.

Dubois, Ellen Carol. "Working Women, Class Relations and Suffrage Militance." In *Unequal Sisters: A Multicultural Reader in U.S. Women's History*, edited by Ellen Carol Dubois and Vicki L. Ruiz. New York: Routledge, 1990, 176–194.

Duke University. "Emergence of Advertising in America," *Duke University, Rare Book, Manuscript, and Special Collections Library*. N.d. http://scriptorium.lib.duke.edu/eaa/ (February 10, 2007).

Ellis, Pearl Idelia. *Americanization through Homemaking*. Los Angeles: Wetzel Publishing Co, 1929.

Erdman, Andrew L. *Blue Vaudeville: Sex, Morals and the Mass Marketing of Amusement, 1895–1915*. Jefferson, NC: McFarland & Company, 2004.

Gabaccia, Donna. *Seeking Common Ground: Multidisciplinary Studies of Immigrant Women in the United States*. Westport, CT: Praeger, 1992.

Golden, Eve. *Anna Held and the Birth of Ziegfeld's Broadway*. Lexington: University of Kentucky Press, 2000.

Holme, Bryan, comp. *The Journal of the Century*. New York: Viking Press, 1976.

Holme, Bryan, and Katharine Tweed, eds. *The World in Vogue*. New York: Viking Press, 1963.

Kibler, M. Alison. *Rank Ladies: Gender and Cultural Hierarchy in American Vaudeville*. Chapel Hill: University of North Carolina Press, 1999.

Killingray, David, and Howard Phillips. *The Spanish Influenza Pandemic of 1918–19: New Perspectives*. New York: Routledge, 2004.

Kitch, Carolyn. *The Girl on the Magazine Cover: The Origins of Visual Stereotypes in American Mass Media*. Chapel Hill, NC: University of North Carolina Press, 2001.

MagazineArt.org. February 6, 2007. http://www.magazineart.org (February 10, 2007).

Makiel, Theresa S. *The Diary of a Shirtwaist Striker*. Ithaca, NY: ILP Press, 1990.

Marzolf, Marion. *Up from the Footnote: A History of Women Journalists*. New York: Hastings House Publishers, 1977.

McConnell, Curt. *A Reliable Car and a Woman Who Knows It: The First Coast-to-Coast Auto Trips by Women, 1899–1916.* Jefferson, NC: McFarland Publishers, 2000.

Miller, Alice Duer. *Are Women People?* New York: George H. Doran, 1915.

Mizejewski, Linda. *Ziegfeld Girl: Image and Icon in Culture and Cinema.* Durham, NC: Duke University Press, 1999.

Morris, Lloyd. *Postscript to Yesterday: America—the Last Fifty Years.* New York: Random House, 1947.

Moses, L. G. *Wild West Shows and the Images of American Indians, 1883–1933.* Albuquerque: University of New Mexico Press, 1996.

Pascoe, Peggy. *Relations of Rescue: The Search for Female Moral Authority in the American West, 1874–1939.* New York: Oxford University Press, 1993.

Peters, Margot. *The House of Barrymore.* New York: Knopf, 1991.

Philipp, Alfred O. "Chicago Folkstuff, Vaudeville." *American Life Histories: Manuscripts from the Federal Writers' Project, 1936–1940.* N.d. http://memory.loc.gov/ammem/browse/ (February 10, 2007).

Piess, Kathy. "Putting on Style: Working Women and Leisure in Turn-of-the-Century New York." In *Women's America: Refocusing the Past*, edited by Linda K. Kerber and Jane Sherron De Hart. New York: Oxford University Press, 1995.

Rabinovitz, Lauren. *For the Love of Pleasure: Women, Movies, and Culture in Turn-of-the-Century Chicago.* New Brunswick, NJ: Rutgers University Press, 1998.

Richardson, Dorothy. *The Long Day: The Story of a New York Working Girl, as Told by Herself.* New York: Century Co., 1905. Available online in Open Collections Program. "Working Women, 1800–1930. *Harvard University Library.* February 8, 2006. http://pds.harvard.edu:8080/pdx/servlet/pds?op=f&id=2597696&n=18 (March 7, 2007).

Riis, Jacob A. *How the Other Half Lives.* New York: Dover Publications, 1971.

Riordan, Teresa. *Inventing Beauty.* New York: Broadway Books, 2004.

Robbins, Trina. "The Day of the Girl: Nell Brinkley and the New Woman." In *New Woman Hybridities: Femininity, Feminism and International Consumer Culture, 1880–1930.* Edited by Margaret Beetham and Ann Heilmann. New York: Routledge, 2004.

Ross, Ishbel. *Angel of the Battlefield: The Life of Clara Barton.* New York: Harper & Brothers, 1956.

———. *Ladies of the Press.* New York: Harper & Brothers, 1936.

Ross, Steven. *Movies and American Society.* Malden, MA: Blackwell Publishers, 2002.

Ruiz, Vicki L. *From Out of the Shadows: Mexican Women in Twentieth-Century America.* New York: Oxford University Press, 1998.

Sanchez, George J. "'Go After the Women': Americanization and the Mexican Immigrant Woman, 1915–1929." In *Unequal Sisters: A Multicultural Reader in U.S. Women's History*, edited by Ellen Carol DuBois and Vicki L. Ruiz. New York: Routledge, 1990, 250–263.

Sanger, Margaret. *An Autobiography.* New York: W. W. Norton, 1938.

Scott, Linda. *Fresh Lipstick: Redressing Fashion and Feminism.* New York: Palgrave Macmillan, 1994.

Sheppard, Alice. *Cartooning for Suffrage.* Albuquerque: University of New Mexico Press, 1994.

Slide, Anthony. *Lois Weber: The Director Who Lost Her Way in History.* Westport, CT: Greenwood Press, 1996.

Sochen, June. *Enduring Values: Women in Popular Cultures.* Westport, CT: Praeger, 1987.

Techman, Howard. *Alice: The Life and Times of Alice Roosevelt Longworth.* New York: Prentice-Hall, 1979.

Thomas, M. Carey. "The Passionate Desire of Women . . . for Higher Education," In *Women's America: Refocusing the Past*, edited by Linda K. Kerber and Jane Sherron De Hart. New York: Oxford University Press, 1995, 273–275.

Time Life Books. *This Fabulous Century.* Vol. 1. New York: Time Life Books, 1969.

———. *This Fabulous Century.* Vol. 2. New York: Time Life Books, 1969.

Truman, Ben. C. *History of the World's Fair: Being a Complete and Authentic Description of the Columbian Exposition.* Philadelphia: Standard Publishing Company, 1893.

Weston, Mary Ann. *Native American in the News: Images of Indians in the Twentieth Century Press.* Westport, CT: Greenwood Press, 1996.

Wharton, Edith. *A Backward Glance.* New York: D. Appleton-Century Co., 1934.

———. *House of Mirth.* New York: Penguin, 2000.

Yandell, Enid, and Laura Hayes. *Three Girls in a Flat.* Chicago: Bright, Leonard and Co., 1892.

Yung, Judy. "The Social Awakening of Chinese American Women as Reported in *Chung Sai Yat Po*, 1990–1911." In *Unequal Sisters: A Multi-cultural Reader in U.S. Women's History*, edited by Carol Ellen Dubois and Vicki L. Ruiz, 195–207. New York: Routledge, 1990.

———. *Unbound Feet: A Social History of Chinese Women in San Francisco.* Berkeley: University of California Press, 1995.

Zeiger, Susan. *In Uncle Sam's Service: Women Workers with the American Expeditionary Force, 1917–1919.* Ithaca, NY: Cornell University Press, 1999.

Zitkala-Sa. *American Indian Stories.* Lincoln: University of Nebraska Press, 1985.

———. " . . . This Semblance of Civilization," In *Women's America*, edited by Linda K. Kerber and Jane Sherron De Hart. New York: Oxford University Press, 1995.

Further Reading and Websites

BOOKS

Aronson, Virginia. *The Influenza Pandemic of 1918*. New York: Chelsea House, 2000.

Coetzee, Frans, and Marilyn Shevin-Coetzee. *World War I: A History in Documents*. New York: Oxford University Press, 2002.

Coyne, Jennifer Tarr. *Come Look at Me: Women in Art*. Palm Beach, FL: Lickle Publishing, 2005.

Dommermuth-Costa, Carol. *Woodrow Wilson*. Minneapolis: Twenty-First Century Books, 2003.

Feldman, Ruth Tenzer. *World War I*. Minneapolis: Twenty-First Century Books, 2004.

Gourley, Catherine. *Good Girl Work*. Minneapolis: Twenty-First Century Books, 1999.

——. *Society's Sisters*. Minneapolis: Twenty-First Century Books, 2004.

Kendall, Martha E. *Failure Is Impossible!: The History of American Women's Rights*. Minneapolis: Twenty-First Century Books, 2001.

Miller, Brandon Marie. *Dressed for the Occasion: What Americans Wore 1620–1970*. Minneapolis: Twenty-First Century Books, 1999.

Otha, Richard Sullivan, and Jim Haskins. *Black Stars: African American Women Scientists and Inventors*. New York: John Wiley, 2002.

Steen, Sandra. *Take It to the Hoop*. Brookfield, CT: Twenty-First Century Books, 2003.

Whitman, Sylvia. *Get Up and Go!: The History of American Road Travel*. Minneapolis: Twenty-First Century Books, 1996.

WEBSITES

The American Variety Stage
http://memory.loc.gov/ammem/vshtml
This Library of Congress website is a multimedia anthology focusing on various forms of popular entertainment, especially vaudeville, which thrived from 1870 to 1920. Included are scripts of plays, theater playbills and programs, motion pictures, and photographs.

Class Distinction
http://xroads.virginia.edu.
A detailed discussion of class distinction and attitudes toward the wealthy summer residents can be found at "Class and Leisure: America's First Resort," created by the American Studies Department at the University of Virginia.

Historic American Sheet Music
http://scriptorium.lib.duke.edu/sheetmusic
The Rare Book, Manuscript, and Special Collections Library at Duke University holds a significant collection of nineteenth- and early twentieth-century American sheet music. The Historic American Sheet Music Project provides access to digital images of 3,042 pieces from the collection, published in the United States between 1850 and 1920.

Influenza Epidemic of 1918
http://www.stanford.edu/group/virus/uda
Known as Spanish flu, or La Grippe, the influenza of 1918–1919 was a global disaster. Stanford University's website provides detailed information about the pandemic, including images, graphs, excerpts from medical journals of the time, and additional contemporary sources, such as letters written by survivors. The site has links to other pages about the virus.

The Triangle Shirtwaist Factory Fire
http://www.ilr.cornell.edu/trianglefire/default.html
The Kheel Center at Cornell University provides extensive primary source documents on the tragic fire, including newspaper articles, eyewitness accounts, trial transcripts, photographs, and editorial cartoons published at the time of the tragedy.

Working Women, 1800–1930
http://ocp.hul.harvard.edu/ww
Harvard University's website *Women Working, 1800–1930* focuses on women's role in the U.S. economy and provides access to digitized historical, manuscript, and image resources selected from Harvard University's library and museum collections. The collection features approximately five hundred thousand digitized pages and images, including manuscripts, books, pamphlets, and photographs.

Index

Photo Acknowledgments

The photographs in this book are used with the permission of: © Bettmann/CORBIS, pp. 3, 9, 14, 19, 20 (bottom), 29, 31 (right), 39, 46, 47, 53, 54 (left), 57, 65; © Kean Collection/Hulton Archive/Getty Images, p. 4; © Roger Viollet Collection/Getty Images, p. 6; Library of Congress, pp. 7, 8, 13, 15, 17, 27, 30, 37, 42, 45 (all), 49, 51, 54 (right), 56, 59, 61, 63, 64, 67 (right), 68, 70, 73, 75, 77, 78, 79, 86, 87 (left), 89, 91, 93, 94, 96, 99, 100, 102, 106, 108, 113, 114, 115, 118, 119, 120, 121 (both), 122 (both), 123, 126, 129, 131, 134; © Stock Montage/Hulton Archive/Getty Images, p. 10; © CORBIS, pp. 16, 20 (top), 83 (left); Mary Evans Picture Library, pp. 22, 109; The Dorothy Dix Collection, Austin Peay State University, p. 24; American Philosophical Society, p. 25; © Elias Goldensky/George Eastman House/Hulton Archive/Getty Images, p. 31 (left); © W. and D. Downey/Hulton Archive/Getty Images, p. 32; © Cynthia Hart Designer/Corbis, p. 33; Bryn Mawr College Library, p. 34; © Swim Ink 2, LLC/CORBIS, p. 36 (both); National Museum of American History, Smithsonian Institution, p. 40; Special Collections, University of California Library, Davis, pp. 48, 124; Image courtesy of The Advertising Archive, p. 58; National Air and Space Museum, Smithsonian Institution (SI 2001-1000), p. 62; Rare Books Division, The New York Public Library, Astor, Lenox and Tilden Foundations, p. 67 (left); © PEMCO-Webster & Stevens Collection; Museum of History and Industry, Seattle/CORBIS, p. 71; Courtesy of Allen County-Fort Wayne Historical Society, p. 74; © Brown Brothers, p. 80; The Granger Collection, New York, pp. 83 (right), 103; © Hulton Archive/Getty Images, pp. 85, 87 (right), 90, 111, 127; © Lewis W. Hine/Hulton Archive/Getty Images, p. 95; © Time & Life Pictures/Getty Images, p. 105; © Branger/Roger Viollet/Getty Images, p. 116; © PoodlesRock/CORBIS, p. 125; © Blue Lantern Studio/Corbis, p. 132.

Front cover: © Hulton Archive/Getty Images (left); © Topical Press Agency/Hulton Archive/Getty Images (right)

About the Author

Catherine Gourley is an award-winning author and editor of books for young adults. A former editor of *Read* magazine, Gourley is the national director for Letters About Literature, a reading-writing promotion program of the Center for the Book in the Library of Congress. In addition, she is the curriculum writer for The Story of Movies, an educational outreach program on film study and visual literacy in the middle school developed by the Film Foundation, Los Angeles.

Among Gourley's more than twenty books are *Media Wizards* and *Society's Sisters* as well as the other four volumes in the Images and Issues of Women in the Twentieth Century series—*Flappers and the New American Woman: Perceptions of Women from 1918 through the 1920s*; *Rosie and Mrs. America: Perceptions of Women in the 1930s and 1940s*; *Gidgets and Women Warriors: Perceptions of Women in the 1950s and 1960s*; and *Ms. and the Material Girls: Perceptions of Women from the 1970s through the 1990s*.